Helping Teens Succeed in High School & Life for Parents & Teachers

Helping Teens Succeed in High School & Life for Parents & Teachers

How High School Shapes a Teen's Future
& What We Can Do to Help Them Thrive

Matt Jones

A **Teacher Saves World!** Book
2020

For contact information, visit **TeacherSavesWorld.com**

ISBN: 978-1-7354948-1-4

For Laurie,
who forever improved my trajectory

Author's Note

I am a teacher. Since 2000, when I got plucked out of my substitute teaching job and given an emergency teaching credential by my first principal because I answered "Yes" to the question "Do you know math?," I've been fortunate to work with thousands of students at five different schools, in five different school districts, in five different towns. I have taught every core subject at some point in grades six through twelve, several elective courses, coached volleyball and basketball, been an Activities Director and Yearbook Advisor, and was even a Vice Principal of Summer School (just once!). I have had to obtain several teaching credentials to do this, and I earned a Master of Arts in Teaching, Multicultural and Social Justice Education. It has been an incredible journey, one I am still on, and I have had my eyes wide open for the entire ride.

Teaching has consumed my thinking for the better part of two decades. Thankfully, my beautiful and extremely patient wife entered the profession with me, and we have been able to spend most evenings and car rides discussing education and all its adjacent topics. We have spent the bulk of our life together teaching at the same school, which has allowed us to move most of our discussions beyond the general and into the specific. We love the arts, sports, travelling, and being outside, especially with our family, but most of our conversations find their way back to the same topics: teaching, parenting, and the development of young people. These conversations eventually became our podcast, Teacher Saves World! that we started in April 2020 while being sheltered in place and teaching remotely. We were not being facetious when we came up with the title—we truly view the act of helping young people develop as the most important act on the planet.

Everything you will find in this book is the result of two decades of teaching with my eyes open and processing what I see with my teacher wife. It's also been influenced by countless articles and books, many about education, but many more on topics that in some way address our basic human desire to live our best life, like habit development, leadership and management, cognitive science, psychology, and character. Even fiction has played a role, as stories are studies of people, their decisions and actions, and the consequences that follow. Where possible, I have given specific credit to those whose research and wisdom I have included in these pages. I have also tried to make it clear when I reference, in a general sense, the research or wisdom of others. In my attempt to gather twenty years of learning, observing and thinking about education, I did not have the ability to specifically cite everything I have ever consumed on the subject. If you read something that you feel needs more specific credit and you know its source, please email me. See the appendix for contact information. I stand on the shoulders of giants, and they deserve all the credit for improving my view.

I am not a clinical psychologist either, although I love to dress up as one in many of my conversations with Laurie. That character also finds its way into these pages. Understanding the motivation and underlying causes of why teenagers do what they do, and the consequences of those actions is at the core of being a middle and high school teacher. By and large, teachers are trying to get large groups of teenagers to do work they would rather not. Being a psychologist, albeit an uncertified one, is a crucial part of our mission. Like soldiers on the frontlines that are cross-trained in basic medical techniques in order to supply life-saving triage where it's just not practical to have a bunch of doctors standing around, teachers supply counseling and assess motives all of the time to achieve their goal of saving young lives. That being said, while the assessments and predictions I make here are based on many years of observing patterns of behavior and their consequences, and reading and coursework on child and human development, I don't have letters after my name that indicate I'm an expert in the field. If you ever feel that your teenager or one that you work with needs more professional support, please find an expert to help them. I list some resources in the appendix, and many are free.

Lastly, the opinions and prescriptions expressed on these pages are mine. They are what I believe to be true, and they are what I have witnessed to be the most effective and efficient methods for improving the life outcomes of teenagers based on all of my observations, experiences, and research. That being said, we are talking about human beings. Unlike computers that can be programmed to do what you want them to, teenagers are emotional beings that have a whole host of influencing factors, from their environment and peer group, to their gender and income level. They also have distinct personalities, representing some mix of nature and nurture. Being a parent of teenagers has increased my respect for the awesome power of nature. While I have worked with and lived in communities that represent a broad swath of humanity, from the ridiculously wealthy to the frighteningly poor, from the privileged insiders to the migrant outsiders, and while much of what I talk about represent truths that transcend all of these barriers, there's no denying these filters have varying levels of distortion on their effectiveness. Each parent and teacher, be them of the classroom variety or any other adult that works with young people to improve their trajectory, will know their teenagers and adjust accordingly. It is what we do.

Contents

Introduction:
HIGH SCHOOL, a HERO'S JOURNEY

"I think one of these days," he said, "you're going to have to find out where you want to go. And then you've got to start going there. But immediately. You can't afford to lose a minute. Not you."

From *The Catcher in the Rye* by J.D. Salinger

The Hero's Journey is a classic story structure where the protagonist sets out in search of something important to them, like a treasure or an elevated position in life, but in order to claim it they must overcome many obstacles. They will have to fight dragons, cross oceans, and solve riddles that will push them to question whether the quest is worth it, daring them to quit and return to their familiar, pedestrian way of life. The challenges they face along the way are designed to test their character and examine how they respond, adapt, and grow. Each challenge will be unique, but together they develop all the facets of character needed for a successful life as a hero. Heroes must be brave *and* smart, strong *and* flexible, theoretical *and* practical. The challenges cannot and should not be easy to achieve because it is not an Average Person's Journey, it is a *Hero's* Journey! There are important questions that need to be answered. Are you worthy of the title of hero? Are you an improved version of your former self? Are you ready to lead an exemplary life as a result of the wisdom and strength you developed on the journey? Has your life trajectory significantly improved as a result of the quest? Are you prepared to make the world a better place by using the skills you developed on your journey? The world needs heroes, lots of them, and heroes are developed, not born. The Hero's Journey, while a literary device, is mirrored in real life, where our real stories, and our real heroes, come from.

We have all experienced one or more of our own Hero's Journeys, periods of heightened challenge that forced us to respond in a way that changed us, hopefully for the better. Our journeys differ in length and complexity, in whether we face them alone or as part of a group, and they differ in their origin. Some journeys are the result of an unexpected life moment, like a death in the family, the loss of a job, or a highly contagious virus. Others are institutionalized, baked into our societal structure to shape its citizenry to the benefit of us all. Without a doubt, the most important one of this variety is high school.

The mythology of high school is real. It has long been fertile territory for coming of age stories, where teenagers stand at the precipice of adulthood and question whether they're ready for the jump, or whether they would rather stand there, frozen in time, forever unburdened with all of life's demands and daunting unknowns. High school is designed to get the teenager unstuck, to propel them confidently into the future they desire. We need them to succeed, otherwise society begins to erode, and we drive away from the fast food joint with an incomplete combo meal because putting a burger *and* fries in the bag was too complex of a task. I should not have to check the bag before driving away! High school happens at a time of epic convergence, where first love collides with puberty[1], learning to drive battles with learning to say no, and advanced forms of math compete with advanced releases of the latest Netflix series. In just four short years, young people will encounter more physical, emotional, spiritual, and intellectual challenges than they have

---

[1] This is likely the reason my fries were missing, as the boy responsible for packing the bag got distracted by the cute girl that just walked up to the counter.

in the previous fourteen. It is arguably the most exhilarating four year stretch in anyone's life. And when they are done? Sorry, but there is no period of rest to soak in the adulation of a successful journey when high school is over: adulthood awaits!

While the Hero's Journey requires that the hero go the entire distance, overcome all the obstacles, and grow into a new and improved version of themselves, they never do it alone. It is impossible. There is always a mentor, someone that has gone through it and provides timely guidance, occasional bursts of motivation, and a kick in the pants when needed. Frodo was the hero, but without Gandalf he does not have a chance to return the ring to Mt. Doom. Harry Potter is just a kid with a scar were it not for Dumbledore. Could Katniss win the Hunger Games without Haymitch's coaching? Likewise, our teenagers going through high school, a real-life Hero's Journey, need mentors now more than ever. Like Gandalf, Dumbledore, and Haymitch, these mentors need to be wise in their advice, tireless in their support, and patient above all else. Teenagers will fall and struggle, and they will be foolish and ungrateful, but mentors are ready for it, and mentors know their heroes in the making are worth it.

They also know that a world void of heroes is not a future they can tolerate.

The world is changing rapidly. It is more global, more connected, and more instant than ever before. What used to take a year now takes a day. What used to produce five now makes a hundred, requiring less time and manpower to do so. Competition is becoming fiercer by the day as more and more applicants become qualified for colleges, rental apartments, and entry level jobs. Yesterday's hero is considered average today. But this is nothing new: it is the way of the world. As the population grows and technology becomes more intelligent, so do the expectations for what makes a hero. As the expectations grow for heroes, so do the expectations for their mentors.

Teachers and parents of teenagers are working harder than ever to support tomorrow's heroes. But are they working smarter, more efficiently? Have they forgotten that a hero is not a hero if their mentor completes the challenge for them? Recent scandals involving wealthy parents going to extreme and illegal lengths to ensure college entrance for their children is shining a bright light on this question. While the world has changed since we teachers and parents of teenagers went through high school, the challenges have purposefully remained intact. While some of the bells and whistles are now more digital than analog in nature, the challenges still test our teenagers in ways that will produce the character traits necessary for a successful, happy life. While how we each define success may vary, the character traits most often associated with successful, happy people have gone unchanged for centuries, maybe forever.

In this book, I distill decades spent working with, observing, researching, reading about, interviewing, and thinking deeply about teenagers and their journey through school, particularly high school. I've traced the lives of individual students and friends, following their journey after high school, then going back to their performance in high school to find commonalities and decode the connection between life after high school and the four years spent within its halls. To say the connection is strong may be an understatement. As I will touch upon shortly, one is rarely surprised by the adult life of someone you knew in high school.

This is a guidebook for mentors. It reminds us of what it means to be in high school, what the demands of the journey are, and how best to support our teenagers in their quest to become the heroes of their own lives. It provides insight, advice, and warnings. It shows you the map, provides the directions, and denotes the hazards along the way.

I will lay out the ten challenges that all teenagers will face in high school and provide insight to both teachers and parents on how best to support their successful completion. I will provide insider, frontline information, as well as the habits exhibited by the most successful heroes. These ten challenges have been around as long as there has been high school, but while some of the rules or tools needed to complete them have changed slightly to keep up with the demands of the time, baseball is still baseball. As you read through the chapters it will evoke memories of your time as a teenager, and in your desire to become a better mentor, you may learn some things about yourself. You may finally come to realize why certain parts of your life journey have not been exactly what you would like them to be. It may be that you never fully completed a challenge. It is never too late!

If after reading you feel that you are not ready to be a mentor, or that maybe it doesn't fit into your busy schedule, then I suggest you find someone you trust that will step up, immediately. Teenagers are going to head out on the journey, and they are going to look for a mentor to guide them and show them the way and fill them with the confidence needed to succeed. In the absence of someone that truly cares for them and looks out for their best interest, they will turn elsewhere. Unfortunately, our world is littered with unscrupulous "mentors" looking for lost souls to lead further astray.

The Four Most Important Years

I remember being at a friend's house in high school, and there was a group of us just hanging out, being high school boys. I believe I was a junior. We were probably listening to the Talking Heads, or maybe Run DMC on cassette in an oversized boombox. Maybe we were farting on each other's heads. There was probably a wedgie or two administered. We might have been arguing over who the hottest Charlie's Angel was[2]. Most likely we were doing all of these, simultaneously. At the most awkward moment possible, my friend's mom walked in. But instead of looking disgusted, she appeared wistful, and as she took in the completely juvenile scene exclaimed, "Enjoy it! High school is the best four years of your life."

Several years later I looked back on that event while I was in college and realized my friend's mom did not go to college because it was way more fun than high school. But for some reason that moment stuck with me, in a sad way. It seemed as if I was party to a confession of a failed life, or at least a life of regret. I felt my friend's mom at that moment was

---

[2] I always argued for Jaclyn Smith. Farah Fawcett was too easy.

contemplating a life that had apparently gone downhill past age eighteen. I never talked about it to my friend, whose mom had, in the presence of all his buddies, discounted his birth and childhood as something less than taking algebra and going to the prom. At some point I let it go and chalked it up to a sad midlife episode from a woman who may have been drunk at the time.

Fast forward thirty years and I am now a high school teacher, and for the past twenty years I have worked with thousands of teenagers in both middle and high school. I started in the solidly middle class neighborhood of my youth, and then moved on to work in a private school that charged more in tuition for a single year than my entire bachelors *or* masters degrees cost and counted the children of Hollywood stars in its student body. I have now spent over a decade on the other side of the train tracks, working in one of America's poorest congressional districts. I have seen young people go off to Ivy League schools and other elite institutions. I have also seen them go to prison, learning of their fate through stories on the evening news or in the local newspaper. I have seen students start and grow flourishing businesses, and had others die before they made it to their 21st birthday. Students from both sides of the tracks have achieved all of these, just not equally. The profession of teaching has imbued me with profound joy *and* deep sadness. It has lifted me up *and* punched me in the face. I could not imagine doing anything else.

I remember clearly in my first year as a teacher feeling as if I was learning too much about the students I served. I found the interaction with students to be so enlightening, the exposure to so many families, through their students, shockingly raw. The way students dress, write, communicate with their peers, approach their studies, and relate to their teachers creates, over time, such a deep and detailed picture of who they are and where they come from. I almost felt ashamed that I knew so much. Over time you come to understand it's part of the gig, a very necessary part. Any mentor must know their future hero deeply. It is in getting to know them and where they come from that you discover the hero that lives inside of all of them. The first part of becoming an effective mentor is believing in this maxim, that there is a hero in each of them that just needs to be developed.

But recently my friend's mom and the comment she made popped into my head.

"Enjoy it! High school is the best four years of your life."

Thirty years later, after her naive (or maybe drunken) statement, I may now believe she was closer to the truth than I gave her credit for. I would just make a little tweak:

"Enjoy it! High school is the *most important* four years of your life."

There is a reason there are so many movies and television shows set during high school. It is a period of titanic development and discovery, a time where we begin to experiment with adult-like freedom and responsibility while still redeeming many of our childhood free passes. We are driving, dating, earning and spending money, all while sleeping in the same bed in the same room we did when we were seven years old, our threadbare blankies keeping us warm and soothed. It is a time when so much of who we are settles in and begins to assume its final shape. We discover and become aware of our personalities, and what other people find attractive and repulsive about us. We develop reputations. Our character takes shape, and as they say, character is destiny.

I am not suggesting that high school is like cement that hardens just before you leave. We all, hopefully, continue to evolve and grow with time, dependent on the amount of reflection we commit to life. Unfortunately, we all know those non-reflective types that are essentially their high school self in an adult body. The path established in high school is disproportionately responsible, good or bad, for a good part of the life journey you take afterwards. At the very least, high school will establish where a teenager will begin their life as an adult, and all you have to do is witness the incredibly large mass of humans that gather to run the Boston Marathon to understand that where you start a race matters. The trajectory of life and performance in high school are intimately linked, and you can choose to see that as unfortunate, or as an opportunity. The most respected parents choose the latter, doing everything in their power to ensure their children master their high school quest and enjoy a successful launch into adulthood. Those that choose the former, do so at their own, and their children's peril.

High School Reunions

High school reunions are an opportunity for people that graduated at the same time from the same high school to get together and catch up on how life is going. I have been to three of these already, and it is always a blast to see how people have evolved and what life journey they are currently on.

There is an interesting dynamic to the event—everyone in the room knew each other when they were young. They played sports together, took tests together, ditched class together, went to dances together, and so on. It is fun to witness first loves reuniting, and watching their current loves try to contain their jealousy! Everyone knew each other when they were young and goofy kids doing all the stuff that young and goofy kids do. This room full of adults were all kids at the same place at the same time. They have a shared history, and they know what that history is. More importantly, they do not just know what everyone in that room did, they know who they were. They were there when the seeds of their character started to take shape.

When you know who someone was in high school, you are rarely surprised by what happens in their adult life. As you move through the room and you catch up with this person and that one, hearing about what's been going on in their life for the last ten years, in the back of your head you're connecting their past to their present, and it almost always makes perfect sense. Not in a way that you could have predicted it—there's just too many possible life outcomes for that—but in a way that is plausible.

"Did you hear, Sarah got a promotion to Vice President?"

"I heard Tom didn't come because he was too embarrassed. He's unemployed, *again*."

"Xavier just bought a house...his third!"

"Patricia just had her 4th child, all from different fathers."

In the age of social media, these revelations will not be spaced out in increments of five to ten years, and maybe reunions themselves will eventually dissolve as the need to reconnect becomes an antiquated idea in our hyperconnected world. Maybe all of these life moments we used to have to wait for the next reunion to hear about will just be included in everyone's social media feed in real time, but the idea is the same: you're rarely surprised.

Why do I spend time thinking about these things? Because eventually people are going to hear stories about my teenagers, stories that will not surprise them. I am a mentor for my two teenage children, and to the hundreds of high school students that I teach and work with every year.

What stories are people going to hear about them in the future that will not be surprising? Moreover, what can I do to be a positive influence on those stories?

Why Now?

It is true that I could have written this book ten years ago, fifteen maybe. It did not take long to pick up on what was working and what was not for students in school. There were also periods in the last ten to fifteen years that would have been much easier to sit down and write a book than the period I find myself in now.

I am sitting down now, finally, because next year our son will be a senior and our daughter a freshman in high school. I am in the thick of it.

Our children have very different personalities, each with their own distinct strengths and challenges. Being a parent of high school aged children has made me a better teacher of other people's high school aged children, and I would like to think my years teaching high school has influenced, for the good, my parenting.

But my wife and I are far from perfect[3], and like most parents we struggle with exactly how to handle situations, when to bring down the hammer or wrap our arms around them, when to be strict or lenient, or when to interpret something as malignant or benign. Parenting is extremely challenging work, and the parenting of teenagers may be the most difficult of all. To anyone reading this book that is parenting a teenager too, know that we are there with you. The fact that both of us are high school teachers might lead you to think parenting teens is a breeze for us, yet we constantly marvel at how often we feel lost and inadequate in our dual-teacher classroom of two as compared to our day jobs where we're alone with over thirty sets of eyes to direct. I remember when our children were younger and needed our constant attention, always wanting to talk about such childish topics like dinosaurs and puppies. I could not wait for them to be teenagers, mini adults that would be able to have more advanced and mature conversations. My life would slowly return to the evolved life of dinner parties and stimulating conversations with other independent and responsible humans that just happened to be my offspring. Oh, the folly and selfishness of my relative youth.

Lastly, I am writing this book shortly after turning fifty, and while I am not a big milestone birthday person, this is one that inspires deeper than normal contemplation. While I have now successfully completed the ten challenges that are the main thrust of this book, I had not when I was graduating from high school. I had completed some, more than half probably, but I struggled with a few important ones. Upon reflection, I can see how my trajectory was impacted by not successfully completing all ten challenges and gathering the character traits associated with each one. I do consider myself successful, and there is little I would change, if anything, about my current station in life.

I just wish I had gotten here sooner.

---

[3] To be fair to my wife, we are not equal in our distance. If "perfect" was the name of our favorite band, she would have front row seats when they came to town, while I would be relegated to the nosebleed section.

I know now that my failure to fully develop myself in the ten challenges meant that I would need to spend time after high school, in college and beyond attempting to master them. I would experience some delays[4], go through many trials and many errors, before achieving the contentment that John Wooden, the former UCLA men's basketball coach and one of the most revered teachers of all time, spoke of when he said, "Success is peace of mind which is a direct result of self-satisfaction in knowing you did your best to become the best you are capable of becoming."

I do not want you to stress out thinking that if your child does not commit to developing these habits that their life is over and nothing but misery will follow. Just know that it might take them a little longer, but that achievement of their best self is still possible, and you and they should never stop working towards that end. That goes for your development too. Do not forget, the mentor, while not the main character in the story, goes through their own transformation as well. There is nothing like teaching to remind you of what you do not know and what you need to learn and how you need to grow. If you are lucky like me, your thirteen-year-old teenage daughter will regularly update you of your shortcomings, usually during dinner when guests are over. Be calm, chew and swallow, and take note. She is probably right.

I would like for my children to spend more of their time on this earth living their best life, and less of it fumbling to get there. I would like for them to write their book earlier in life than I did, and I would like for them to produce more of them than I will have time to.

I want that for your children too.

The ten challenges are designed to help your student become their best self, and ultimately that is the goal. There is probably nothing that frustrates mentors more than squandered potential, but we must make sure we do not confuse a child's potential with our own preferences and

---

[4] I spent the first seven years after high school in college, and no I am not a doctor, thanks for asking. My teaching credential and master's degree came years later. All told, I have spent around fifteen years in college, and no, I am still not a doctor, so stop rubbing it in.

desires. We often get in trouble and sour our mentor-hero relationship when our "high expectations" cross over into "destination of our preference."[5] So please, do not focus on the outcomes (grades, positions earned), and do not fall into the comparison trap ("How did Susan's kid get into Dartmouth?"). Also, beware of the bubble you live in and whether the voices echoing inside it match what your family defines as successful. Focus on what you know in your gut really matters, what is really going to make a difference in their life moving forward. When we're able to get to a quiet place where the loud voices in our bubble are no longer ricocheting all around us, and we can think clearly with our head and heart about the life we hope for our children, we usually come back to their character. We want them to be decent and hardworking, brave, smart, have good friends, and have a positive outlook on life. The ten challenges of high school are designed to produce just that.

---

[5] If you need a refresher on this dynamic, just watch any movie where the parent's idea of what the child should become is different than what the child wants to do, creating the central conflict of the film and setting up an emotional ending where they reconcile once the parent realizes the error of their way. *Billy Elliot* is one of my favorites in this genre.

Chapter One

The First Challenge:
GET HEALTHY

People got used to anything their bodies gave them; he was no exception. If your body was well, you expected it to perform for you, excellently, consistently. If your body was not, your expectations were different.

From *A Little Life* by Hanya Yanagihara

I t all starts with wellness: physical, emotional, mental and social. It is the source of our energy to keep us focused and alert. It gives us the confidence to tackle new challenges. It gives us the strength to do the work we need to do and want to do. It fights off diseases that try to bring us down, and it repairs the parts damaged by those bugs that get past our initial defenses. It provides a sense of belonging, letting us know we are not alone in this world. How far we go, how deep we dive, and how long we last are all a result of how well we are. Can you ignore this challenge and still experience success? Maybe, but while the "flawed hero" has become the norm in our Marvel-ized world, the "unhealthy hero" is not something anyone aspires to or promotes, even comedically. Heroism relies on health.

While we must work with the body we inherited, with its unique set of strengths and weaknesses, there is much we can do to make sure it is running in top form. Our teenagers' health and wellness will be challenged on all fronts, being asked to get up and perform earlier than they would like, to focus for longer than they believe they can, and to work with people they would rather not. This is the initial challenge because it asks the question, "are you strong enough to get through this thing called life?" We need our teenagers to build their capacity for handling all that life demands, and that is going to be hard to do if they cannot work or focus for any length of time. Even worse, they cannot accomplish anything if they are always home because they are sick.

We adults understand well the impact of physical, emotional, mental and social wellness on our ability to accomplish what we desire in life. We watch television shows and listen to podcasts dedicated to the topic. We join gyms and read books to improve our health. We overhaul our pantries and obtain memberships to organizations that promise to help us improve our most important statistics. We share our regimes with other adults, comparing results and seeking guidance on tweaks we can make to get ahead. We investigate whether the life hacks work, and we download apps to utilize current technologies to help make us healthier.

Teenagers, not so much. They are eating and drinking more calories than ever before, and those calories are emptier than ever before. They are less active than ever before, and they have a greater ability to be mean to each other on a grander scale than ever before. Make no mistake, these are challenging times to be a teenager. They are surrounded by beautifully packaged and easily consumed foods and drinks that are full of highly addictive and awful junk, and devoid of any redeeming nutrients. They are deluged by apps and games purposefully engineered to take advantage of their brain's susceptibility to addictive content. They are unwittingly being marketed to more than ever through social media and its "influencers," keeping their wallets in a constant state of depletion. It is the rare teenager that has the self-awareness to see past all of this to make the healthy choices they need to make to improve their health. Mentors play a larger than normal role in this challenge.

This is a high-impact challenge, one that bears greater on future outcomes than some others do. The habits and attitudes we develop in high school surrounding our health stick with us, usually for life. Changing bad habits in this area proves hard to do, but when accomplished can significantly improve a person's trajectory. I think we can all agree, especially anyone that has struggled in their adult life to get a handle on their health, that getting this figured out in high school, establishing and then taking good habits and attitudes about health and wellness into adulthood is the desired course of action.

Sugar is a Poison

Do not take this as hard science, but my gut-o-meter says 80% of the problems encountered by teenagers would be solved if we could get them to eat decently and sleep more. There has been speculation from those that know way more than I do that the current generation of children may be the first ever to have a shorter life expectancy than their parents. If our goal is to help our children achieve a success greater than or equal to our own, then simply making sure they live as long or longer than we do is where we need to start.

Teaching as a profession includes a certain youth elixir bonus. Being constantly in the company of young people and their youthful exuberance has a buoying effect. Like a pinball careening around a pinball machine, the teaching day can be a wild ride. That pinball finally sinking down into the hole signifying game over is a pretty good approximation of how I feel every day at the final bell. While I mostly feel young in this job, when it comes to this topic, I feel incredibly old fashioned. I dream of turning the clock back, way back, to the good old days when kids ate oranges and drank water, in a glass, from the tap. If you were outside, the garden hose worked just fine.

The current generation of teenagers are under assault from highly addictive elements that are shortening their life span. There is no way a child can think and grow to their best self if we do not help them get some basic contributors to their development, mainly eating and sleeping, back to healthy levels.

Let us start with eating. Somewhere in the late 1970s there was a shift in the food industry, and that shift introduced massive amounts of sugar into the foods we eat, particularly the processed foods that dominate the shelves and freezers of our grocery stores. Some experts have gone as far as to call sugar a poison, and like the fight against nicotine previous generations had to wage, a large-scale war against sugar is needed quickly to save a generation. Only this one is worse because we all eat, unlike previously when only smokers and those near them were affected. This is impacting *everyone*.

You picked up this book and you are reading, so you are not clueless. You know that childhood obesity is skyrocketing, that the number of young people being diagnosed with Type 2 Diabetes is skyrocketing, and that the number of children being prescribed medication to moderate their health and moods is also, you guessed it, skyrocketing. It is up to us, and by us, I mean parents and teachers of young people, to do something about the assault being waged on our children's health and wellness.

This is one of those areas where we as adults need to put our adult pants on, be strong, be loving, and do our job. When I see students at school with backpacks that resemble a magician's bag, where a never ending stream of chip bags and candy are pulled out of them and devoured by teenagers I'm tasked with getting to focus and learn, my grandpa rage kicks in, and I start shaking my fist at those darned kids pumping themselves full of sugar. Something I always must remind myself of is *it is not their fault*. Just like the rabid compulsion felt by addicts, teenagers' need for sugar is crazy strong.

For the sake of your child's health and their ability to think and focus during a long school day, you need to get on top of a few things. You are going to get pushback, that is for sure, and you are going to find wrappers from devoured junk food under their bed, but you are the parent, so parent. Here are a few suggestions:

- Make sure they eat breakfast every morning before school, and preferably not something super sugary like most cereals. Toast with peanut butter, fruit, oatmeal, eggs, and milk are all decent options.
- Keep your pantry as free as possible of chips and other individually packaged snacks that are easily stuffed into backpacks. Try to transition to snacks that are lower in sugar like nuts and cheese.
- Have them drink way more water and try to eliminate or significantly reduce consumption of sugary drinks like soda, energy drinks, flavored teas, and most blended concoctions peddled by "coffee" houses.
- Eat as many meals together, as a family, as possible.

We could go much deeper on this topic, but there are tons of information out there if you want more, including many great documentary movies on outlets like Netflix and Amazon Prime[1]. Simply making healthy eating a priority in your house is the best thing you can do, and once you do that, you will find the proper steps that match your family's goals.

Establishing proper eating habits is a gigantic leap towards improving our teenagers' health, but I believe it will only get us about halfway to where we need to get. Establishing proper sleeping patterns is the other half of the journey, and just like how our children's waistlines and hearts are under attack from sugar, their sleep is under attack from something no other generation has had to deal with: personal technology devices.

---

[1] *What the Health* on Netflix and *Fed Up* on Amazon Prime Video are worth checking out.

Technology is Teenage Heroin

It is time for me to get my grandpa slippers on again and start shaking my fist. Nothing gets me going like those darned kids and their electronic devices!

You do not have to be that old to remember a time before everyone had a cellphone. If you are like me and you grew up before they invaded earth, you can remember when it was time to come home, it meant that you were *home*, and you could relax into, well, just being at home. I can remember doing my homework not because I wanted to, but because I was bored and had nothing else to do, so why not. It helped fill the time between coming home and going to bed. I am old enough to have grown up before On Demand and DVRs, so I could not even watch a TV show until it was scheduled to air. Does anyone still do that? Being home used to be a relaxing place for our teenage brains, a place removed from the distractions and dramas swirling in the teenage universe. While all teenagers desperately want to spend as much time as possible with their friends, prior to the cellphone invasion we all eventually had to come home and disconnect from them, and it allowed our brains to relax and focus on things like homework, talking to our parents, and maybe doing a few chores. Those times are gone.

Technology, and cellphones in particular, has made it so that teenagers never have to be separated from their peers. Through social media, they are in constant contact with each other, and they are constantly influenced by what they see and hear on their phones. They're spending less and less time being influenced by adults that care about them, adults that are modeling mature behaviors that teenagers are expected to be developing, and they are spending more time in the company of those that do not truly have their best interest in their hearts, and exhibit moronic behaviors that keep our young adults stunted and immature. It is a really hard time to be a parent.

But we cannot forget, it is a really hard time to be a kid, too. Again, it is like the food thing—*it is not their fault*. These technologies are purposefully engineered to be addictive, and you know we would be the same way if these things were around when we were young.

There are some things we can and should be doing to reduce technology's negative impacts on the development of our kids. I am by no means anti-technology—I am not composing this on a typewriter, and you probably purchased this book on Amazon. Technology has a place in our society, but there are some places it needs to get out of, namely our kids' bedrooms.

At the high school I teach at, we have gone one-to-one (one device for each student) with Chromebooks. Many schools have gone this direction, many with Chromebooks, but I also know of iPads and some other laptops being used. The idea is great—many books are now digital, reducing their backpack load, and it ensures that *all* students have access to the advanced educational tools of the day. There are also many generous programs out there that provide internet access free of charge to those that otherwise could not afford it. Technology can be a great equalizer, democratizing opportunities and opening doors. As someone that earned their master's degree in Social Justice and Multicultural Education, I find these aspects of technology important and exciting.

As a parent and teacher, I also see their potential to do extreme harm.

Parents seem to be all over the map when it comes to monitoring their child's technology. I know that there are those out there that are constantly monitoring and tracking their child's whereabouts and online activity, and there are others that have no idea what is going on. Some do not allow any social media, while others just blindly pay the bill. You need to figure out what is best for your family, but I will say that I have found extreme measures usually lead to extreme responses. Complete prohibition can lead to sneaking and lying, and complete freedom can lead to irresponsible gluttony. I find moderation is usually the best course to take. If you are like me, you would be perfectly happy with some cataclysmic event wiping out forever the existence of cellphones and the internet, but we all know that is just a dream we old and cranky people share. Technology is here to stay, and we need to, like every other advancement that has scared the bejesus out of the elders, find a way to help our young people handle it responsibly.

The easiest and best way I know and have seen that works is to simply apply limits. If your children are going to get their homework done and they are going to get enough sleep, which for teenagers is 9 hours a night on school nights[2], we should all be taking these measures:

- Have a buffer on both ends of their day, after they wake up and before they go to bed, where access to cellphones is not allowed. Allowing them to wake up and have a good breakfast before getting online is a good idea for the morning, and requiring that their phones "go to bed" one hour before their actual bedtime is a good end of the day practice.

- Do not have TVs and video game systems in their bedrooms, and do not allow *any* devices to be charged and left in there overnight. Their bedroom is a place that they need to sleep, deeply, and devices only disrupt that.

- Have a period immediately after they get home where cellphones are turned off and homework and/or chores are completed before they get back online. Odds are they have spent a lot of time on them during the school day, permitted or not, and a little decompression time sans technology is healthy for the soul. It is likely they will need to use a device to do their work, but what can you do? There are only so many moles you can whack. Do not give up—whack the moles you can.

---

[2] The American Academy of Pediatrics recently urged middle and high schools to move back start times to 8:30 am or later to allow teens to sleep more. A study found 87% of high schoolers were not getting sufficient sleep, and consistent lack of sleep can lead to attention, behavior, and learning problems, along with having a negative impact on physical health. Not good if you are trying to complete a Hero's Journey.

- For teachers, I would encourage giving the parents of your students an assist by limiting how much screen time is required to get your homework done. I know it's very easy to drink the Kool-Aid and take advantage of all of the buzzy tech tools available to educators these days, but think about the parents that might not have as much filtering control at home as you do at school. "I have homework" has become easy cover for "I want to watch YouTube."

I either just validated your current good practices, or I just set you up for a huge battle with your teenager if none of those things are happening in your house and you plan to do something about it. Sorry if the latter is true, but the fact that you're reading this shows that you want what's best for your teenager, and in the same way we want our child to put forth the work to meet their potential, we need to be willing to do the same. It'll be hard to make the change, but I guarantee it will be worth it when your child is finally getting the sleep they need and are performing at a level well beyond their currently sleep-deprived and frazzled brain could ever imagine.

Get Involved

Abraham Maslow was a psychologist that developed his Theory of Human Motivation on the belief that in order to reach self-actualization (the fulfillment of one's potential), certain basic needs must be met first. In my observations and experience, I find the theory to be largely accurate, and because school is a place where the goal is to help children along their journey to self-actualization, the levels required to get there are present on every campus.

All humans need food and shelter. Schools have always provided both, and the school's place as an integral provider of nutrition for young people has become increasingly prevalent in the last decade. In fact, one of the main concerns of schools shutting down during the COVID-19 pandemic was the meals they provided to their students. While in person instruction was largely shut-down, schools continued to provide grab-and-go meals to the communities they serve. Schools understand; you cannot reach your potential if you are hungry.

We also need to feel safe. Unfortunately, this need has been under assault in the last twenty years, and schools have responded through increased security measures and anti-bullying campaigns. Technology has also introduced a new platform for threatening behaviors to flourish, and schools are finding that many if not most physical, on-campus altercations are starting on social media. Schools are constantly trying to employ the latest technology to thwart these negative influences, from camera surveillance systems to anonymous tip-lines and text numbers.

Humans also thirst for for love and belonging, the need to know we are not alone in this world. It is here where high schools really ramp up their game.

High schools are extremely active places beyond the school day. Drive past any elementary or middle school, and they are largely quiet and empty not too long after the final bell. High school campuses keep humming, well into the evening and on most weekends. Even during the school day, there exists a whole world of events and activities happening beyond the classroom. I believe this to be the magic sauce that makes high school such a special place—almost everyone, and many for the first time, find their tribe and that sense of belonging.

It is well known and deeply supported with research that students that get involved do better academically than those that do not. Some of it has to do with a need to do better or they will not get to participate. A little pressure is good that way. Most of it, however, has to do with that third level need to belong. School is no longer just an academic prison but an exciting place where students get to align themselves with students that have similar interests. They get to spend many hours with those new friends practicing and displaying their developing talents. The greatest memories most students have of high school are the bus rides with their basketball teammates, the day spent hanging out at a band competition, or the hours spent rehearsing for the school play. It is not the algebra lesson or the history project.

Students that are involved in school through sports, clubs, performing arts, or any of the many opportunities to get plugged in are just happier and better students. In this whole book, it is one of the items I feel strongest about. In my experience as a teacher *and* as a high school student, I know that academic performance and involvement in school are intricately linked. It is not a guarantee that they will make the honor roll, but their academic performance will be better than if they were not involved in anything.

Whatever it takes, get your student involved in *something*. It will truly make a world of difference.

Find the Positive

There is no denying that the teenage years are dramatic. The surging emotions, the exposure to a broader swath of what exists in the world, new ideas exploding in their brains and hearts, and radical new levels of relationships. It is a wildly exciting, confusing, and at times heartbreaking time. The highs are touching the stars, and the lows are scraping muck off the bottom of the ocean. There is no joy like high school joy, and there is no drama like high school drama.

It is important in this time to help our students moderate these emotions, and to help them foster a positive disposition. Positive thinkers see the possible in situations, they are more apt to find solutions to problems, and they are less prone to fall into pits of despair. Positive thinkers are more likely to have positive relationships, and they are more likely to have friends, period. People like to be around positive people.

Do not confuse positive with bubbly or talkative. Introverts can be just as positive as extroverts. It has less to do with their outward personality and more with how they perceive life's events. Here is an example:

Imagine you are driving down a crowded freeway, and your car is full of guests from out of town and you are all headed to a sporting event. Ahead of you and one lane to the right you notice a large hubcap dislodge itself from the front left tire of a very old and beat up sedan, miraculously slice itself through traffic, careen off of the cement median, and launch into the air, heading directly at your windshield. Your life flashes before your eyes as you envision the hubcap crashing through your window. Instead, you make a subtle shift to your right, staying in your lane because the lane to your right is full of speeding cars, but enough to move the car far enough to the right so that the hubcap is no longer hurtling towards your head but instead slices off your driver's side mirror. Minus a side mirror, you and all your guests make it to the sporting event[3].

Once you get home, how would you describe this event to others? Think about it before moving on.

A positive thinker's response would be something along the lines of, "You won't believe what happened to me today! I was driving to the game with my friends from out of town when out of nowhere this hubcap comes hurtling right at my head! Luckily, I was able to move just enough so that it took out my side mirror instead of my windshield. I'm just glad nobody got hurt and we were able to make it to the game."

A more negative response would sound something like, "You won't believe what happened today! I am driving to the game with my buddies, the freeway was jam packed, and out of nowhere this hubcap comes flying at my head. It ended up slicing off my side view mirror, can you believe it? Of all the cars on the freeway, I am the one that gets hit! As if the game was not expensive enough, now I have to buy a new side mirror too!"

See the difference? Can you hear these two different responses in people you know?

The first response is from a person that has a habit of finding the good in the world, and the second in finding the bad.

If you sense that your child may have a negative leaning personality, fear not, it is changeable. The best way I know to do this is through

---

[3] This happened. I was the driver.

simply expressing gratitude on a regular basis. Gratitude journals are a great way to accomplish this and doing it as a family is even better. Try it by using a basic notebook, and on the first page write today's date at the top and draw lines to divide the page into boxes so that each family member gets a box. Either when everyone is together, like at the meal table, or separately if such a time does not exist, have everyone jot down three things they are grateful for. Anything in the world, big or small. Keep doing this every day.

What happens through this practice is the increased noticing of good, positive things in the world. At first, it is an assignment— *"Ugh...I have to write three good things down. I better look for something to write."* Soon the forced assignment becomes a habit and finding the good in the world becomes the new normal. You also have this great family notebook that is fun to flip through when you need a little boost on a grey day.

Go for a Walk

A good, brisk walk, outdoors, free of technology, can be a powerful tonic for the body, mind, and soul.

Let's face it. Walking is not taken seriously as exercise, especially these days in the age of super high intensity workout crazes. It can be massively intimidating to have a gym membership and step on the treadmill at a walking pace while everyone around you is furiously pushing their bodies to extremes that cause them to collapse to the ground in such complete exhaustion that just a few seconds more would have required someone to call 9-1-1.

The health benefits of walking are often overlooked, and just 30 minutes a day can make a significant improvement on a person's health. But the great thing about walking is that it benefits more than just our physical health—it has benefits for the mind and soul as well.

Walking has long been revered by our great thinkers to dislodge ideas stuck in the dark recesses of their mind. Walking, especially outdoors, allows our mind to wander and loosen up, freeing thoughts and ideas that have been clenched up and muted from the stresses of the day. "Aha" moments are common during walks because walking releases the tension of stressful periods spent trying to solve or understand something, and a relaxed brain is an incredible machine. If you or your student ever have a long session of mental application, like working on a project or a particularly challenging set of geometry problems, just a ten minute break in the middle spent going for a walk can loosen the mind and make the second half go quicker and more successfully.

Walking also soothes the soul. Whether we do it alone and allow ourselves to ponder what's going on in our lives at the moment, or with a loved one as an opportunity to catch up on their life, time to reflect and process the goings on around us is necessary to reduce stress from building up. In a period when our teens are beginning to pull away from us, developing a regular walking routine with your teen, even just once a week, could be a great way to stay connected.

For the mental and emotional benefits of the walk to be most effective, you need to do this walk without your phone. Keep the earbuds out of your ears, listen to the world around you, take in your surroundings, put one foot in front of the other, and feel the stresses and worries and unsolved problems evaporate. Let the mind wander, and as it does, receive the thoughts and ideas that float to the surface, the solutions to problems you previously believed unsolvable.

Please, Step Up Your Grooming Game

High school is challenging enough for the well-groomed. For the pungent and greasy, it can be downright brutal. Additionally, body odor is a little like second-hand smoke: those nearby are also affected.

Eighth grade is usually where we start to see students caring about how they look. There are always those early adopters, kids in elementary school that dress and groom themselves better than some of your adult co-workers, but oftentimes they're the result of a meticulously groomed parent that also has a touch of OCD and can't bear to see their little angels with a hair out of place. Middle school is where we start to really see self-motivated grooming and dressing, and we (parents) start to find it difficult to see ourselves in the mirror because our children are camped out in front of them.

While diet and exercise get all the attention on the health front, being clean is often overlooked. Grooming, the act of caring for and styling those parts of our appearance that the general population are exposed to, is an extension of cleanliness, and it's this whole package that I want you and your student to take seriously.

Please make sure the rock bottom basics of hand washing, teeth brushing, and deodorant applying are being done religiously at the appropriate times. The next level of care includes regular bathing and attention to the body, specifically the hair and skin, with extra attention given to the skin of the face. Please take the time to learn about the specific needs of your child's hair and skin, and get the appropriate products and regimes going. This includes boys! Teenagers' bodies are going through such radical changes, and these changes, if ignored, can lead to odors and textures nobody wants.

Lastly, the clothes they wear, their personal style, starts to really take shape in high school. During the teenage years, an important part of our development is the establishing of our own personality distinct from our parents. Teenagers start to pull away and assert independence[4], and part of that is choosing what to wear. What they choose will often align with the tribe they have started associating with. It is a complicated dance they are learning—the establishment of a unique identity within the norms of the group they have chosen to be a part of.

I do not want you to feel like you need to take out a second mortgage and get your kid a whole new wardrobe and line of hair and skin products. There are always deals to be had. But the bottom line is we're trying to help our children perform at their best to be their best, and we can all agree that when you look good, you feel good, and when you feel good, you are more likely to do good.

---

[4] Causing many moms and some dads to feel like they have been broken up with.

A student that feels self-conscious about their appearance is not likely to be focused in class. A student confident in their appearance, is free to soar.

Wrapping It Up

Physical Education is one of the many courses I have taught, and I would often start the year off by informing my students that this may be the most important class they take in all high school. I was working with freshmen, and confused faces would develop, and I could interpret the inner dialogue that was taking place—*"PE? Important? Did Mr. Jones not take his medication this morning?"* I would then go on to explain that I was not referring to the course itself, but what it represented in relation to everything else they would learn during their four years. It represented a commitment to being healthy, and any hope of becoming their best selves and utilizing everything they were going to be learning in their other courses would be heavily influenced by their health.

Remember Wooden and his idea of success being that peace of mind derived from doing your best to be your best? I know that some of you may be wondering why you know of some obviously unhealthy people that seem to be doing better than some very healthy people. First, what we may be perceiving on the outside may be very different from what's going on behind the scenes, but let's for a moment, take it at face value and ask the question, *"how can an unhealthy person be more successful than a healthy person?"* It goes back to Wooden.

The goal is not to be better than someone else, but to be our best self. The two people you may be comparing in your head—the unhealthy successful one and the healthy unsuccessful one—would most likely be in very different positions if their health changed. Who knows how much more the unhealthy one could achieve were they to achieve optimum health? And the healthy one would possibly be much worse off were their health at lower levels.

The road to success is more effectively travelled with a healthy body, mind, and soul. This is the first challenge because commitment to our children's health will impact all the others. Let us make a commitment together, as parents and teachers of young people, to ensure this generation continues the upward trend of life expectancy.

The Challenge's Impact on Trajectories

Here and for the next nine chapters, in this section I offer glimpses into the possible life trajectories of students that have complete, moderate, or no success with that chapter's challenge. I went with an aviation theme, calling them Ready for Take Off! (complete success), Still Boarding (moderate success), or Flight Delayed (no success). Scoring ten Successful Launches is a super rare feat, and not something you should expect from your teen(s). Most of us leave high school with a mix of results, continuing to work on those we are deficient on into adulthood. The hope is to avoid collecting any Flight Delays and strive for a mix of Successful Launches and On the Runways that hopefully favor the higher end.

Ready for Take Off!

The student that leaves high school with healthy habits, a decent grasp of proper eating and exercise routines, an appropriate level of self-esteem and confidence, and a robust social life with quality relationships, is primed to make the most of life after high school. Healthy people make a great first impression, and there is no arguing the value of first impressions in getting ahead in life. Strong social skills and confidence open many doors, and increased levels of energy from good nutrition and exercise allow them to take advantage of those opportunities. Healthy individuals will also experience fewer avoidable illnesses, limiting their time calling in sick and missing out on important work or events. They will rebound quicker from the illnesses they do get. Healthy relationships also mean reduced drama and stress, as well as increased support in challenging times. Strong social networks can also be leveraged for advancement. Their positive attitude makes them attractive and fun to be around, increasing their chances of meeting the kind of people that make for good life partners. Surrounding themselves with other healthy and positive individuals has a multiplying effect on their trajectory, enhancing an already good life. Healthy people not only live a longer life, but they wring more out of each day they are alive.

Still Boarding

So many students are highly active in high school, but that does not always translate into being healthy. Raging teenage metabolisms and active practice schedules often mask unhealthy habits that make themselves instantly visible when metabolisms decrease, and sports no longer mandate exercise (hello freshman fifteen!). An increased waistline is normal if it does not reach unhealthy levels. It's likely these students' background and memories of younger days spent running and jumping in ways unimaginable in their current condition, will push them to attempt to recapture some of that youthful vigor, prompting them to explore better nutrition and exercise routines. This may lead to periods of fad diet exploration and a strained relationship with their bathroom scale before finding their groove. On the social and emotional fronts, these students may be hampered with a little more self-doubt or social anxiety than you would hope for, causing them to hold back when others are surging forward. It is not so bad as to make them avoid situations altogether, but just enough to keep them from finishing first or going all the way. It could be the difference between being considered for a leadership position versus a spot on the team.

Flight Delayed

The chronically unhealthy high school student is in for a lifetime of setbacks. For the physically unhealthy, reduced energy levels and mobility equate to missed opportunities. Sickness is often their normal state, and their unreliability erodes the trust other people have in them to be counted on. There are obvious fiscal and longevity issues too when it comes to extreme levels of poor health. Poor emotional development can cause many problems after high school. Being unprepared to handle the complex social dynamics of the adult world can lead to tragic outcomes, the worst of which is a complete avoidance of the adult world altogether. An underdeveloped or non-existent social network can lead to feelings of isolation, deepening or heightening any fears of involvement. Unfortunately, there exist too many opportunities for these students to feel they are living a fulfilled life, albeit virtually through video games or online communities, allowing them to ease into these situations instead of encouraging them to fight their way out. Maybe that is a good thing, but its value is lost on me.

PD for Parents & Teachers

PD is short for Professional Development, something we teachers receive loads of. At the end of each of the chapters that detail one of the ten challenges, I offer up some PD for parents and teachers in the form of suggestions for how to apply what was presented in this chapter at home or in the classroom. It presents a sampling of the actions we can take to support our teenagers on their Hero's Journey.

For Parents

- Reduce sugar consumption! Systematically swap out most of the individually packaged and sugar laden snacks our children are devouring in alarming quantities for healthier options like nuts, cheese, and fruits and vegetables. Drink more water, too.
- Put restrictions on technology use and get all devices out of the bedroom and out of their hands for at least the first and

last hours of the day. Use these limits as a springboard to establish regular nighttime routines that ensure your child is getting the required 9 to 9.5 hours of sleep. Start with their wake-up time and count the hours backwards from there. By the 9th hour prior to waking up, they need to be asleep, which is not the same as going to bed. The technology free hour spent prior to falling asleep should be dedicated to calming and relaxing activities, like reading.

- Check the school website, talk to a counselor, or attend any orientations that will inform you and your student about what extracurricular activities are offered. Encourage them to get involved in activities that match their interests and support their involvement by offering to transport them as needed and by getting involved in parent booster groups associated with their activities.

For Teachers

- Announce, post in your classroom, and encourage all opportunities for students to get involved with extracurricular activities. When possible, make targeted suggestions for students to get connected, matching their talents and interests with clubs or groups you think they would enjoy. Students, especially freshmen, are often unaware or afraid to get involved, and encouragement from their teachers goes a long way. Be a good model by getting involved yourself as an advisor or participant in school wide events like rallies and try to support your students that are involved by watching them perform or compete. Catching just one game after school means a lot to them. They always notice when teachers show up.
- Maintain a healthy classroom. Water is always encouraged, and maybe healthy snacks, but candy and other unhealthy

food and drink should be banned. Do not hand out candy as a reward—it sends a conflicting message, and the reward itself is a motivation killer. Keep your physical space healthy as well, by keeping it clean and organized, and promote healthy interactions through community building activities.

- Use technology wisely. Make sure, when used, that the focus is on learning content and building skills. Block what you can and be vigilant in your monitoring. When personal devices like Chromebooks or iPads are not in use, have them be put away and out of sight to reduce students' temptations to login and tune out.

Habits that Work for Teenagers

The following represent examples of good habits displayed by students that successfully master this challenge. These habits can be altered by changing the cue (the time or event stated in the first half) and/or the cue response (the action stated after the comma that was set off by the cue) to meet the specific needs of the student's life and school reality. This is true for this section in all future chapters. The habit appears first in bold, with an explanation of its value that follows it.

- **At 8pm each school night, I will turn off any personal devices and plug them into their charger outside of my bedroom.** By establishing a regular time that electronic devices are shut down each school night, students can develop regular routines for unwinding and getting proper sleep. Also, by making sure their bedroom is free of devices that go buzz and beep in the night, they will be able to get to sleep more quickly and achieve longer and deeper levels of sleep.

- **Every Monday morning, I will check the school's events calendar to see what I can attend or get involved with.**

By regularly checking school calendars, announcements, emails, or whatever way their school shares information, students get plugged into the wide array of events going on. Many schools also utilize social media to keep their students and families informed. Knowing when auditions for the play are, when tickets go on sale for the dance, when soccer try-outs are being held, and when and where club meetings are being held ensures a student doesn't miss out on an opportunity to get plugged in and feel like they belong.

- **Every evening after dinner, I will take a walk around the block and think about the good things that happened that day.** Walks are not strenuous, but they are an effective way to move your body and clear your mind. Also, by making it an opportunity to reflect on the positive happenings of the day, the ability to see the good in what goes on around us every day becomes stronger. This could be a great whole family habit as well.

Chapter Two

The Second Challenge:
GROW UP

"The problem with growing up," Quentin said, "is that once you're grown up, people who aren't grown up aren't fun anymore."

From *The Magicians* by Lev Grossman

The change from freshman to senior year is seismic. In this time, they go from being kids that rely on their parents for *everything*, to young adults that are beginning to explore a new land of independence and responsibility. Their bodies assume new shapes and sizes, as the growth factories inside of them go into overdrive during these four years. Like the effect a full moon has on a werewolf, hormones take over their brains, causing parents to consider locking them in their rooms until the moon has recessed. Unfortunately, the moon seems to linger in the sky indefinitely. They begin to date, drive, work, and venture out on their own in high school, but in short bursts for practice. In order to eventually do it for real, without the safety net of a free place to sleep and eat, they are going to need to mature, big time.

This challenge will have a significant influence on how much of this new territory is open to them, largely because certain echelons require a

35

level of sophistication purposely intended to filter out the less mature, the less ready. This challenge will also govern how they manage and grow wealth as an adult, as it is in this challenge that they learn to strengthen and effectively deploy their stores of willpower. This challenge, as sobering as it sounds, may also be what determines which side of the law they land on.

The increased levels of independence high school students experience are unleashed on them immediately in freshman year. Researchers have noted that the freshman year of high school is one of the most turbulent transitions in a young person's life, and one that derails many journeys before they ever get started. While this book is dedicated to how high school impacts a teenager's life trajectory, if I were to focus on just one year of high school, it would be freshman year, hands down. It is not even close or up for debate. This one year is more influential than the other three *combined*.

How students handle freshman year, with its radically relaxed structure compared to the rather draconian middle schools[1] they just exited, is a super-duper strong indicator of how they will finish high school, and I do not use duper lightly. The degree of change in the academic performance exhibited by students during their four years of high school, either up or down, is on average incredibly small. Academic performance in high school is largely a flat-line, so getting that flat-line as high as it can possibly be their freshman year is super-duper important. Again, the duper should let you know how serious I am. And their performance prior to freshman year, while not nothing, is not as impactful as you might think. Many high school districts are finally waking up to this fact and have begun to develop programs specifically aimed at supporting freshmen, knowing that how they finish this year is likely how they will finish high school.

---

[1] Middle schools need to be draconian, trust me. I spent my first eight years of teaching at this level, and without the rigid structures in place, our nation's population would be significantly less. Middle school teachers deserve combat pay.

So, what is it about high school, and freshman year in particular, that can be so disruptive to a child's development? Glad you asked. It really comes down to two things: independence and workload. The shift from eighth to ninth grade is seismic, not gradual. They are going to experience much higher levels of freedom on campus and in classrooms, and they are going to be expected to handle significantly greater and more complex levels of work than ever before. They are also expected to handle this while they shift from being the ruling class to the newbies. As if all of this weren't enough, their bodies start to change, their hormones kick in, and they are surrounded by young adults three and four years their senior that dress, talk, and act in ways that can be intimidating or exciting, and often both in a burning ball of confusion. If they can navigate all of this, the odds are strongly in their favor that the rest of high school will go smoothly. Finish poorly, and it will be hard to recover.

The increased independence is going to be present everywhere, from the dress code, to the use of cellphones, to the language used, to the teacher oversight and communication with parents. High school teachers, for the most part, have a different mindset than their K-8 cousins. They tend to be more subject focused[2], and preparation for college focused. High school teachers meet and plan in their subject groups, so it's rare for specific student concerns to be talked about because Johnny's teachers never get together to talk about Johnny, they meet with other teachers of their subject to talk about their subject[3]. Parent monitoring and communication with the school and their child's teachers is paramount in freshman year. Do not sit back and wait for the school to call you and schedule a conference—you may need to initiate this process if it is necessary. Hopefully, it is not.

---

[2] Based largely on the different teacher credentialing requirements for high school, which are single-subject specific.

[3] Districts that are trying to reform freshman year performance are changing this dynamic by creating groups of cross-subject teams so that Johnny can be talked about, and Johnny's trajectory improved, sooner.

The system and the teachers mean well, because in their mind they have four years to get these kids ready to be adults, which means being able to handle independence and more work. They also manage a campus that has young adults that are on the verge of being released into this new world and shaping a campus environment that caters to the youngest classes would be a disservice to them. So, independence and more work win out, and the freshmen need to get up to speed and quickly. Helping them adapt to this new environment, seeing it more as an opportunity to be grabbed than something scary to be avoided, will be the mentor's challenge.

High School is a Fresh Start

Whether they realize it or not, students have a reputation at school. Over time, as adults interact with them, see the things they do, hear the things they say, they start to develop an opinion about the kind of person they are. Students may like their reputation, or they may not and feel that it's not true and people just need to stop picking on them and get to know them better (if I had a nickel...), but it is what it is. Every student has one, good, bad, or indifferent.

The reputation I want to focus on is the one they have (or had if they have finished 8th grade) with the adults at their middle school. What do/did the teachers think about them? Administrators? Cafeteria workers? Bus drivers?

Not sure? Most likely, if you are the parent of an 8th grader and you are not sure of the reputation they have, you are in denial, but I'll cut you some slack and honor your confusion. Let's try to clear it up by taking a little survey. You might be able to complete this without insight from your teenager in question. If you need their input, try to do so discreetly. Let us keep the past, especially if it is not humble brag Facebook material, where it belongs.

Below are five statements. Read each statement and give it a score of 1-5, using the following scale:

1- totally disagree 2- disagree
3-neutral
4- agree 5- totally agree

_____ 1. Teachers would call my child's name several times a class, and it was usually to get them to return to their seat or return something that was not theirs

_____ 2. They sometimes had a table all to themselves in the cafeteria because good table manners just were not their thing

_____ 3. The workers in the office all knew their name because they were up there so often, and it was not because he or she was an office aide

_____ 4. I/We (parents, guardians, loved ones) got so tired of calls home from school that I/we blocked the school's number

_____ 5. Your student was often sat next to the best student in the class, and that student was deputized by the teacher to be a helper and redirector

Add up the points and let us see how they did.

22-25 points- Darth Vader. They were a menace, and maybe a leader of other, menace-leaning hellions. The adults all got a little tense when they entered the room, and they celebrated when they were absent.

18-21 points- Storm Trooper. They were not quite menace-leader material, which requires an extra level of cunning and effort, but the adults were equally happy when they were absent. They may have been best friends with a menace leader and followed them to the darkside.

13-17 points- Lando Calrissean. They were conflicted, hybrid personalities. They straddled the line between the dark and the light, usually going where the opportunity was most lucrative or best suited their objectives. Their forays to the darkside were accompanied with a personal anguish that eventually caused them to willfully atone for their sins.

9-12 points- Han Solo. They were mostly good, but occasionally, they did something stupid that hurt decent people, but usually as a result of trying to do something good and they went too far. They were always forgiven and their allegiance to the light was never in question.

5-8 points- Luke Skywalker. They had a good reputation, hung out with good people, were generally innocent, and people associated them with hope in the universe. When a leader was needed, people looked in their direction whether they wanted the job or not.

I am old*ish*, so that is why I went with the original Star Wars characters. If you want newer characters, I'd say Kylo Ren, Storm Trooper, Finn (only at the start of *The Force Awakens*, he then jumps over Poe and joins Rey for the remainder of the final trilogy), Poe, Rey. I love Harry Potter too, so that would be Voldemort, Draco, Snape, Ron, Harry & Hermione.

I gave you a hint in my reputation descriptions about the point that I ultimately want to make here. I used phrases like "they *were* a menace" and "they *had* a good reputation" for a reason: they are in the *past*. While they probably did not just develop this reputation, and these behaviors that earned the reputation are behaviors they have been exhibiting for a while, the truth is they are in the past. They represent the middle and elementary school version of your student.

What is the high school version going to be like?

It is a legitimate question, because you are most likely going to a new school where none of the adults know them. The teachers are not going to cry when they see their name on their class roster, because they do not know them. Their reputation is wiped clean.

This is true for those that like their good reputations too. They will need to establish it, again, but they are used to it. They just need to do what they have been doing.

But high school is an amazing opportunity to start over. It's not easy, but if they (and you!) are tired of people not wanting to sit next to them, or of endless lunch detentions, or poor grades, or of never getting rewards or certificates of recognition, then the effort will be worth it, for all of you.

High school just might be your student's last, best chance at a new reputation. Take advantage of it.

Maturity is Learning to Say "No!"

I spent the first eight years of my teaching life working in middle schools, and then I took a one-year detour to elementary school in a self-contained sixth grade classroom. In my tenth year, I made the leap to high school.

Yes, I said leap. The difference between middle school and high school campus culture is like the difference between a twenty-minute car ride to the store and a five-hour plane flight to Hawaii, minus the tropical setting and perfect climate. Unless the store is in Hawaii, I guess.

The transition from eighth to ninth grade is a drastic one. Students go from being the ruling class where their behaviors set the tone and are emulated by those beneath them, to being seen as children to be tolerated by schoolmates that are driving, working at jobs outside of the house, and grooming parts of their body many freshmen haven't discovered yet. The need to adopt the new set of acceptable behaviors and fully assimilate into their new, more mature surroundings should be a freshman's first order of business. In some ways, the first dragon they will encounter on their Hero's Journey will be an internal one, the need to scream "no!" to all of the immature impulses exploding within them

41

at the most inappropriate times in front of the most intimidating audiences. Sometimes this will be a fire-breathing dragon that needs to be slayed, while other times it will be a wise dragon that presents riddles to be solved with a Queen's English accent. This is part of the challenge; brute force and intellectual prowess are both required, and knowing which to use and when, matters.

Insurance companies extract exorbitant rates from the families of teenage drivers not because they are not skilled at driving, but because they are impulsive, and teenagers are extra impulsive when around other teenagers. California, where I live, has even changed its licensing rules since I was a teenager in an attempt to combat that phenomenon by restricting for a period of time who teenage drivers can transport in their vehicles, knowing that a teenage driver alone and a teenage driver with a *carload of other teenagers* have very different accident rates.

One of the points I like to make to my freshmen students early in the year as I am setting my expectations for their behavior, is to make an appeal to *their expertise*. It is not something they are used to, but it reminds them of everything they already know, and I believe gives them a sense of power over their own life. In simplest terms, this is the goal of high school: getting young people ready to take control of their own lives.

I start off by reminding them that at the very least, a freshman is in their 10th year of school, kindergarten being the first year of compulsory schooling in America. For those that went to preschool, they have even more years of *experience* under their belt. I then ask them what term we use to refer to people that have been doing something for ten years, often citing professional athletes because it is an arena where most students have at least some familiarity. With very little prodding, we get to the concept of a "veteran." We discuss the qualities of a veteran as well as their counterpart, the rookie. As far as being a student goes, and the proper behavior of students, even as freshmen, they are veterans. They know what is *expected* of them. They all have ten or more years of experience with teachers, classmates, homework, assemblies, cafeteria lunches, you name it. There is nothing they do not know about how to be a student. They are experts, now act like it.

You may believe that after this impressive, thoughtful discussion led by a caring, veteran teacher, that an instant transformation would be noticeable. Not only would it be seen in how they sat up a little straighter and folded their hands just so on their desktops, but it would be felt as the collective age of the classroom just took a quantum leap forward, causing a shockwave of maturity to pulse through the room, removing a few wrinkles and stray odors before exiting through the cracked window. My class of freshmen, full of the confidence and freedom of a newly minted group of pre-adults ready to prove themselves on this new stage, would begin to mutate before my eyes and begin to resemble a graduate seminar minus the MacBooks. Yeah, me too, until some kid farts and they all erupt in laughter.

"Rookies," I mumble to myself and shake my head.

Willpower

Willpower, which is also referred to as self-regulation or self-control, has been argued to be the cause of anything good or bad that can happen to a person, beyond the accidental. Great successes like earning a spot in the NBA or starting and growing a flourishing business are only possible through the application of willpower, and ills like incarceration or massive gambling debts result from a failure of application. There is a very strong argument to be made that the level of success anyone achieves in life is proportional to their development and application of willpower. Success in this sense applies to anything that you can make work in life, from having a marriage that lasts to responsibly using credit cards. The more you have and use the higher you will soar, and the less you have and use the further you will sink. If you believe this argument as I wholeheartedly do, addressing your child's development of willpower will be of paramount concern to you.

The good news is that it can be addressed, and wherever your teen is now, they can improve. That goes for all of us, really. Willpower, like many things, is like a muscle; it can be strengthened through exercise and will atrophy through inattention. Like muscle strength, willpower is finite. As the day progresses, we only have so much willpower to apply, and the more we use it the quicker it runs out[4]. So, the greater the stores of willpower we can develop, the more instances we will have it available to apply. Willpower is another reason sleep is so important: our stores are recharged as we sleep. Depriving yourself of sleep is like unplugging your phone with less than a full charge. Students should be heading to school at 100%, but many arrive with less than 50% from sleep deprivation. This is why teachers dread classes after lunch—many students have used up all their willpower and either have a hard time keeping their heads off their desks or resisting the urge to play on their phones.

Willpower can be, like a muscle again, developed through exercise. The systematic application of effort towards doing activities or actions you would otherwise not do, or actively do not want to do, will strengthen your willpower. See this as the act of *saying no to most of your impulses*. Willpower development in children, in my years of working with and observing young people and how their families operate, is one of those high impact character traits that is directly related to parental attention and effort. Take this seriously and work hard to develop it in your children. The "hands off" approach to parenting does its greatest damage here.

Unfortunately, my most immature students are often those that spend the least amount of time under the caring direction of adults, and the most amount of time under the immature influence of peers. Parents, teachers, coaches, and any other adult mentor your child may have is going to expect that your child exhibits more mature behaviors and redirects them when they stray. Their peers will do the opposite[5]. Simply put, the child that has attentive parents with high expectations of

---

[4] Hence the greater likelihood of an argument with your spouse after a long day at work. After using up all your willpower doing work you may not want to do or dealing with ridiculous customers that you do not want to be nice to, an argument with your spouse is more difficult to avoid.

[5] Have you seen the stuff they watch on YouTube and think is hilarious?

behavior, then goes to school with teachers with high expectations of behaviors, then goes to soccer practice with a coach with high expectations of behavior, and all of them redirect this student when they fail to meet those expectations, is going to be significantly more mature than the student that just goes to school and hangs out with their friends and on their phone.

The more they can receive good modeling, high expectations, and redirection and feedback, the sooner these behaviors move from being something that requires them to use willpower and becomes a habit. Once it becomes a habit, willpower is no longer needed and can instead be used to tackle new and greater things. The road to success is built by willpower, one habit at a time.

Here are some ideas for ways you can help your child develop their willpower:

- Have clear expectations of how they should behave and perform. Expectations are one of those deeply researched and effective practices we learn in our teaching credential programs: low expectations lead to low returns, high expectations to high returns.

- Get them involved in activities that require them to learn and grow under the tutelage of a caring adult. Sports and the arts are great for willpower development. Jobs and community service are also opportunities to work under the supervision of adults with expectations of their performance and behavior.

- Reduce environmental factors that unnecessarily require the use of willpower. This is the *do not buy cookies if you are trying to lose weight* approach. If your child needs to focus on getting homework done, you cannot be watching TV in the same room. If they are in their room doing work, their phone should not be with them. (When I write, I make sure to close my email tabs and turn my phone off.)

- Make sure they get 9 to 9.5 hours of sleep nightly

- Do not stop redirecting because you are afraid that you are being a nag. This is tough for parents, especially when you have asked your son a million times to put his dirty socks in the hamper and not the floor. We are playing a long game, and while we do not want to be a jerk or an ogre, we also cannot give up. What we tolerate, we encourage.

To this last point, know that many of the good habits we may have today are the result of our parents nagging us. I can still hear my father's voice in my head when it comes to the quality of my work. Whenever I feel like doing something halfway, I can hear him prodding me to do better, be it how I cleaned the hamster cage or completed my 8th grade Constitution Report. Did I always meet his expectations? No. Did we sometimes get angry with each other? Yes.

Am I a much better person today than I would be if he did not care, and instead of giving me feedback on my hamster cage cleaning or Constitution Report efforts sat in front of the TV and cracked open a beer?

100%, yes.

Spend More Time with Grown Ups

Three years into my teaching career, my wife Laurie and I were expecting our first child. We had purchased our first house in Long Beach, California only a year prior, but something about impending parenthood caused a rewiring of our mental circuitry, and all of the rational and practical centers of our brains were short circuited, and the emotional and irrational centers took it upon themselves to pick up the slack. Even though we each had great teaching jobs and a beautiful home that we had been in for less than a year[6], we *had to move back to Hawaii* and my

---

[6] That house would almost triple in value a few years after we just *had to sell it and move.*

wife *had to stay home with the baby*[7]. So, we put our house on the market, gave notice to our great teaching jobs[8], and moved back into Laurie's childhood home with my mother-in-law, convincing ourselves that somehow this time would be different[9].

Laurie's high school friend Karen was working in a private school on the windward side of Oahu in the town of Kailua, Hawaii, where Laurie had grown up and where we were about to move in with her mother. An interview was arranged, and I obtained a position teaching in the middle school of Le Jardin Academy. I felt like I had died and gone to teaching heaven! I taught half as many students in half as many classes and had twice as much time to prepare and grade. I, along with all of the students in the high school, was issued a laptop that connected via wi-fi anywhere on campus *in 2003*[10], and I was able to use this laptop to work on my classroom's lanai that had a view of the ocean. I was also making half as much money, and Laurie and I had to share a car and live with her mother, but I still count my time at Le Jardin as some of the best years I've had on this earth. The new and different conditions of teaching in a private school, being new parents, and the majestic setting of Hawaii all combined for a magical time, but I want to focus on one thing in particular I learned from observing a major difference between how private and public school kids spend their time.

Private school kids spend much more time in the presence of adults.

There's a socioeconomic component to this, among them that many of the families that send their kids to private school can afford to have a

---

[7] I have absolutely no judgement on this matter, and support those that are able to do it. The emphasis denotes the shift in our thinking from pre to post pregnancy.

[8] We had to leave in May, just prior to the end of the school year because our son *had to be born in Hawaii*. If we had waited until the end of the school year, Laurie would have been too far along in her pregnancy to fly.

[9] We had lived there previously, for a year and half while we got married. Out of respect for my children's incredibly sweet grandmother, the details end here. There are more important things to talk about.

[10] The public high school I work at now would accomplish this in 2016.

parent that doesn't work, and they have more disposable income to pay for lessons, camps, club sports, and other activities. At the school itself, the ratio of adults to students was also significantly different than what is normally found at public schools. All these factors contribute to private school students spending much more time in the presence of adults learning how to behave like, well, adults. It was instantly obvious to me on my first day how different, how much more mature these students were.

I want to point out that these students were not more intelligent than my public-school students, but on average they possessed greater *soft skills*, those abilities like communication and working within a team that employers prize over hard skills. Most companies have elaborate training programs to teach the specific hard skills their business requires, but it's the soft skills that they consistently find lacking in their new hires, and it's this lacking that is the primary reason people lose their jobs. They do not get fired because they are unable to wash windows or fold t-shirts, they get fired because they cannot get along with coworkers or show up on time with regularity.

Public school parents do not despair! There are things we can do to help our kids mature through the regular interaction and caring redirection from adults.

- Find regular time to talk with your kids without cell phones present or the TV blaring. Around the dinner table is great. In the car to and from school is good too. A few minutes here, and a few minutes there goes a long way. Teach them how to make eye contact and speak in full sentences.
- At family gatherings, encourage engagement with extended family, especially family elders, who are often much more formal in their communication because of the era they were raised in. There is much to be learned there. Grandparents are also incredibly patient with young people and truly treasure their time with their grandchildren (often to our

dismay as we witness a person almost unrecognizable as the parent that raised us).

- As noted previously, get them involved in activities that involve the oversight of adults that have expectations of how they behave and will redirect them when they veer.
- When possible, have them handle transactions like ordering food from a waiter or purchasing an item from a cashier.
- Encourage them to make regular contact with their teachers, both in person and through mediums like email, teaching them how to compose mature electronic communications.

To this last point, communicating regularly and maturely with their teachers is an important strategy in their development that will have corollary benefits later in high school. In their senior year they will be asking teachers to write them letters of recommendation for colleges and scholarships, and the stronger the bonds they've created, and the more mature behaviors they've displayed, the more likely their teachers will write exemplary letters. These letters can make a big difference in where they get accepted and how much money they eventually earn.

Kids need to be kids, and it is important that they also have unstructured time to be goofy and get their wiggles out without fear of an adult yelling at them to grow up. But in this very important time, the four years prior to legal adulthood, it is important they learn how to be an adult and get as much good modeling and practice as they can.

Donkey Basketball

Donkey basketball is done as a fundraiser where a local non-profit contacts somebody that has ten donkeys and a basketball referee's jersey. He puts on his jersey, loads the donkeys in a trailer, and heads to the gymnasium that the non-profit has secured[11]. The non-profit organizes

---

[11] By the look of his jersey upon arrival, that is usually the order of events.

two teams associated with the organization, like maybe police versus fire departments, they sell a bunch of tickets, and people show up to watch the two teams play a game of basketball while riding donkeys.

The game would be entertaining if donkeys were compliant animals. Just watching people try to pass and shoot a basketball while riding on the back of an animal is a hoot in itself. The fact that donkeys are not compliant animals makes it a hoot *and* a holler. Donkeys are famous for their stubbornness, and they can give a damn which basket the person on their back wants to shoot towards, and they can give two damns about the score. They seem largely pissed off that the guy who feeds them and occasionally dresses like a zebra makes them wear rubber shoes and wrestle with humans every so often. Donkeys are in no hurry to please anyone, especially if there is no dangling carrot.

Working with teenage boys is a lot like playing donkey basketball.

Anyone that has worked with boys in their early teens, around the time of middle school, will tell you that common wisdom suggests that they should stop going to school for two, maybe three years. They should instead be enrolled in a program that is mostly physical and requires very little if any sitting. This place could be a farm, or maybe a military-like setting. Once it's been determined that they're ready to head back to an academic setting, with its long periods of sitting and focused attention, they do not rejoin the group of girls that moved ahead while they were shoveling hay or repairing helicopters. No, they go back to where they left off, taking the place of the boys two to three years their junior that just left for the farm. This would put them in classes with girls two to three years younger than them. Academically, that would be about right.

Girls and boys are drastically different *culturally* in their approach to school. Girl culture says doing well in school, being organized, and having a bag full of sharpened pencils and overly expensive writing pens *that could supply the entire class* is really, really cool. Boy culture does not agree. Boy culture says backpacks are optional, paper looks cool when it is wrinkled, and sitting up straight is only good for strengthening your abs. If you are a parent of both genders, you know what I am talking about. Laurie and I have one of each, and if you were to walk to the end of the hallway and stand in the space between their two bedrooms with their doors open so that you could absorb both spaces, to not instantly recognize which gender occupied which room would not be possible. I cannot even think of something funny to say about how impossible it would be, that is how impossible it is.

Unfortunately, our school system does not conform to common wisdom, instead mandating that all children, regardless of gender, shall march through the system together with other children all born within a year of each other.

For parents of boys, all I can say is be patient. We love our boys, but like those donkeys that refuse to be nudged in the direction of your basket despite your vigorous tug on their rope, they are less likely to care about pleasing adults as our girls are. It is not disrespectful, and it is not a sign that they do not love us or care about making us happy, it is just that they are boys. Donkeys are donkeys, and to get mad at them for not going in the direction you want them to is wasted energy. It is frustrating, yes, no doubt about it, but you volunteered for donkey basketball. Likewise, if you are working with young men, it is likely something you agreed to.

Our boys, although it seems otherwise much of the time, are no less bright or care any less about their future than girls do. It will likely just take them a little longer to let us see how bright they are or how much they care. It will likely take them longer to believe how bright they are and how much they care about their future. The quintessential boy, Huckleberry Finn, gave us insight into the boy brain when he said, "What's the use you learning to do right when it's troublesome to do right and ain't no trouble to do wrong, and the wages is just the same?" Mark Twain's *Adventures of Huckleberry Finn* was published in 1884!

Teaching and parenting boys requires us to be more patient, more alert, more involved, and more resilient than we sometimes wish we had to be. Our boys are notorious late bloomers, just like I know I was, spending a little longer in college than I probably should have, and taking a little longer to get my footing as an adult than those around me cared for. I am thankful they were patient, knowing that there is a little

Huckleberry in most of our boys, and knowing that there's a good heart and a good brain in there that just needs a little more time to reveal itself.

Wrapping It Up

High school is a truly incredible period of physical, emotional, and intellectual maturation, but the degree and quality of this maturation, in all areas, will be dependent on the effort applied by the child and their caregivers. They will all grow older during this time, but will they become more mature? The two do not automatically go hand in hand. Just think of some adults you know that are highly impulsive, get caught up in social media drama, and can never seem to be serious, instead always cracking jokes and giggling. They act like a teenager in an adult's body, prompting you to look around for the adult trapped in the teenager's body so that a supernatural Freaky Friday event can help explain your weird friend or coworker. Stop looking. They failed to mature but getting older is going to happen whether we like it or not.

This situation I just described is a dangerous one, and it's one I'm sure we all encounter at work (the coworker that sends inappropriate emails or is constantly late to meetings), at the store (the person that walks around having a loud conversation on speakerphone while they shop), or even in our own families (the cousin that's always inappropriately dressed at birthday gatherings). I encounter it all the time through my students' families, and it is a great destabilizing force. I mentioned Maslow's Hierarchy of Needs previously, and I briefly summarized the second level need to feel secure. What I did not mention was that part of the need to feel secure, was the need for stability.

Maturity and stability are intricately linked. One of the sadder realities of my job is working with innocent children that are being raised in chaotic homes, where different forms of abuse may be present, economic instability is ever present, and the oversight of a caring adult is nonexistent. How do you think this child is going to perform at school? It is heartbreaking, and one that causes all of us educators regular anguish (and at times anger) as we try our best to make a difference.

But while I just described the ills of immaturity in the extreme, there are lesser forms that will have lifelong impact if not corrected. While lack of impulse control can lead to a life of addiction, in lesser forms it can mean an inability to save money and a constant reliance on credit cards to handle life's inevitable problems, like needing a new set of tires at the end of the month. It can mean oversleeping one too many times and being let go from a job and a constant cycle of entry level positions and low wages. It can mean multiple unwanted pregnancies. It can mean divorce as a result of infidelity. You get the picture.

We are humans, and we are going to make mistakes. We are going to be impulsive at times, we are going to say stupid things, and we are going to have actions we wish we could take back. This should not, however, be the norm.

Maturity and stability are intricately linked, and stability and success in life are intricately linked. Paying bills, then saving and investing, *then* buying a new pair of shoes takes maturity. Getting that advanced degree in the evenings after a full day at work to earn that promotion and a raise takes maturity. Ignoring the advances of a very attractive coworker out of respect for your spouse takes maturity. Establishing expectations of behavior for your teenager and redirecting them when they stray, you guessed it, takes maturity.

The Challenge's Impact on Trajectories

Ready for Take Off!

The mature high school graduate is an instantly recognizable creature, one that the established adults in the wild are quick to recruit into their pack. The way they stand and communicate, straighter and more confident than the other animals just released into the wild, sends a signal that they are ready. It also establishes them as the future leaders. Their advanced skills in all areas, both hard and soft, are the result of years spent exercising superior levels of self-regulation. This foundation allows them to bypass entry-level positions, or to spend a minimum amount of time there before it becomes obvious, they are ready for more complex work. This faster than normal advancement is not something that gives them pause, as the confidence and comfort they have built up over the years of engaging in adult situations makes their forward movement feel natural. Their personal life also enjoys a greater level of stability, as they can make more mature decisions concerning their finances and health. Savings accounts and investments are started and contributed to early in their life, and their pantry is stocked with healthier foods. They can commit focus to today *and* tomorrow, and as a result both flourishes.

Still Boarding

Our middle of the pack students are ready to be released into the wild, but they are going to leave the safety of their cage just a little more timidly than their more mature and confident peers. Lacking some of the sophistication and refinement of the group above, these students might hold back a little, realizing they need a little more time wandering the streets and observing how others behave and interact, picking up the new lingo and codes of conduct. Lacking a little confidence in their complete knowledge of the new rules, they may stick to their own, congregating with other newbies in a similar stage of development, practicing the new rules and lingo together, safely, before trying to integrate into more mature circles. While this group is mature *enough*, and confident *enough* to fully function in society, they may choose to stay here in this middle pack where, honestly, most of the world exists. There is a microcosm that exists within this large middle, and position within it depends largely on the individual's ability to self-regulate. The difference between an upper, middle, or lower middle-class existence is largely dependent on money management, a domain of life that relies on the manager's ability to show restraint, make good decisions based on solid advice, and to make and stick to a plan. Their ability to exert self-control in the workplace and within their relationships will also factor into their placement within the middle.

Flight Delayed

Our poor teenagers that have spent the fewest hours in the presence of adults, learning what it means to be mature, refining their communication and mannerisms, and building up strong reserves of willpower, are instantly recognizable as the weakest in the herd. They enter the adult world either nervous and scared, understanding instantly their deficiencies as the established inhabitants speak and act in ways extremely foreign to them, or oddly energized, clueless of their shortcomings but excited by the new areas available to them in their adult body. The first group will retreat, running back to the cage they were released from, shutting the door and turning on the Xbox. The second group will be a glutinous scourge, constantly broke and indulgent, these forever teens will be the loud and odorous group that cause us to cross the street a little sooner than we had planned when we see them coming in the opposite direction.

PD for Parents & Teachers

For Parents

- Embrace the fresh start! Whatever was working, continue doing. Whatever was not, stop doing. High school is a chance at a do over, to remake a reputation into something that will lead to a desired adult life. Take the time with your child to reflect on the past, identify the mistakes, discuss the unwanted outcomes of those mistakes, and vow to replace them with behaviors that will make everyone happier.

- Take willpower development seriously. Help them to develop impulse control by setting clear expectations for behavior, redirecting them when they stray, and acknowledging when they succeed. Tweak your environment to reduce unnecessary willpower usage, like turning off or removing unused electronics during homework time, and by having stable and predictable routines around activities like meals and bedtime.
- Get them involved in activities that are under the supervision of caring adults that have much higher expectations of behavior than their peers do. Common ones include sports and the arts, but this could also be a job or a service-oriented activity, like volunteering to walk and care for dogs at the animal shelter.

For Teachers

- Have a willpower friendly classroom, one that has predictable routines, is clean and organized, and limits distractions. The more psychic energy that can be funneled towards schoolwork instead of fighting off the desire to access personal devices, trying to adapt to constantly changing routines, or just generally frazzled by a cluttered and disorganized room, the better your students can commit to focused work.
- Consider flexible seating arrangements, where desks and tables can be shifted between individual and group work arrangements. Asking teenagers to focus on their own work while always sitting in a group is a big ask, and a big drain on their willpower. Teenagers are hyper social and doing a set of math problems while sitting next to friends requires them to both focus on the math and fight off the desire to talk to their neighbors.

- Help students engage in mature interpersonal and presentational communication by both modeling how their speech should sound, and by providing sentence frames and stems, portions of sentences where they fill in content specific information. By first hearing what their speech should sound like from their teacher, and then having a script of sentence frames and stems that allow them to produce mature sounding communication, helps teenagers learn how to speak more maturely. (*They Say/I Say* by Gerald Graff and Cathy Birkenstein is a great resource for this.)

Habits that Work for Teenagers

- **Just before I enter the classroom, I will turn my phone off.** By taking the preemptive step of turning off their phone, students can save an incredible amount of willpower that would have been wasted fighting off the urge to check out all of the inane yet unmissable activity happening online as indicated by the constant vibrations in their pocket. Also, by taking this action themselves instead of waiting for a teacher to remind them, they take ownership of a self-regulation technique they can utilize anytime they need to focus.
- **Whenever I am out with my parents, I will ask if I can help with the transactions.** By regularly engaging in adult world activities like using credit/debit cards to pay for purchases, figuring out the proper amount of tip and adding it to the bill, and asking questions of workers to help clarify a purchasing decision, teenagers begin to feel comfortable handling these situations and will feel more comfortable going out with friends and engaging in these situations on their own.
- **The first time I see my teachers each week, I will ask them a question like, "How was your weekend?"** By

actively generating mature interpersonal communication with adults, teens can start to develop a comfort with those real-world skills. Also, the act of asking someone else about themselves, instead of constantly talking about yourself, is a very mature act. Doing this repeatedly develops a true interest in others, which is a clear signal the teenager deserves to be seen as a young adult.

Chapter Three

The Third Challenge:
SEE the FUTURE

The path to my fixed purpose is laid with iron rails, whereon my soul is grooved to run.

Captain Ahab in *Moby Dick* by Herman Melville

I never read Moby Dick, the epic tale of a captain's obsessive quest to slay the great white whale that bit off his leg. However, it was one of my dad's favorite books, and early in my adult life, when I may have been a little directionless, carefree and adrift on the sea of life shall we say, he wrote the above quote in a birthday card to me. It really grabbed me by the throat when I first read it, its imagery so perfectly capturing the captain's intense focus on his goal. I would come to understand much later that it was a not so subtle message that I needed to find my own iron rails. Better yet, I needed to forge those rails and then hammer them into the earth with long, iron spikes. Once I did, my soul would truly be free to run.

Life's most effective travelers know how to leverage all three phases of their journey, using lessons learned from the past to refine their route, gathering the available knowledge of the moment to keep themselves focused and engaged, all while utilizing the motivating and stabilizing forces of a desired destination. It is the last phase, the future, that if missing can lead to a stalled, errant, or unfulfilled journey. Imagine a balloon full of air that is suddenly untied, the air rushing out, propelling the balloon wildly about the available space, its movements random and unpredictable. Now imagine that balloon attached to a toy wooden car, and that wooden car attached to a string that is taut and fixed at both ends. Once that balloon is released, that toy car will zoom forward along the string until it reaches the other side. That is the kind of impact this challenge has on a teenager's future. Without the string, who knows where the balloon will end up.

The future becomes suddenly real for teenagers just prior to entering high school. In the second half of their eighth-grade year, they start to register for their high school classes that put them on a path to graduate high school and complete their odyssey through compulsory schooling. It is at this moment that life's first big "destination"—graduation from high school, turning eighteen, and becoming an adult—comes into view. After thirteen years as a passenger, having almost every aspect of their life determined by and facilitated by their parents, young teens start to grasp that their journey beyond this first port will be starkly different. They are going to need to learn how to drive *and* navigate, and quickly. While they hope the adults will still be around to instruct and mentor, the fact that responsibility for their voyage's success is transitioning into their hands begins to settle like an elephant on their chest. Or maybe a white whale on their leg is a more apt metaphor.

Students respond to this reality in different ways. Impending graduation from high school signals that the part of the journey dictated by others is coming to an end, and they're going to need to take ownership of their inevitable future and establish some solid ideas of how they want their journey to continue. While some will readily accept this challenge and be energized by it, others will put it off or ignore it altogether. Some will try to stall their momentum, attempting to freeze time and stay on this wonderful island where they experience increased freedoms with limited responsibilities. However, their response, the future is coming.

High school, like Ahab, is obsessive in its quest, and that quest is to prepare teenagers for the future. Students will be surrounded by college educated adults that will encourage them to continue their education after high school. Career Technical Education (CTE) courses will encourage them to explore a desired profession and the skills and training required to earn a position in the field. Teachers will ask students to set goals, both for their courses and for life in general, encouraging students to look ahead and begin the practice of choosing a destination and then charting a course to get there. Counselors will meet with them periodically to update their plans as more of the journey moves to the rear, and what is ahead comes into clearer focus. At the very least, it gets closer.

Helping students understand the relevance of their studies to their future is one of the mentor's primary tasks. "Why do I need to know this?" is a common refrain with teenagers, and "because it is required for graduation," is not a sufficient response. Algebra is not a required course because they might be engineers[1], but because solving algebra problems develops logical and critical thinking, problem solving, abstract reasoning, and step-by-step analysis skills, along with challenging their focus and mental endurance. All of those are relevant to *everyone's* adult life, regardless of what they end up doing. *Everything* they do in high school is relevant to their future, but without the development of a post high school vision, those reasons will be lost on teenagers that are always stuck in the moment. Mentors' patience and restraint will be tested during this challenge, as teens love to pose ridiculous counter arguments to refute a mentor's claim of relevance just to get a rise and exert control. Our ability to delay gratification will be on full display, and we need to be good models.

Being able to formulate a desired future supplies boatloads of motivation. How motivated is a kid that wants to get to the next level of their favorite video game? *Very!* They are willing to practice, read,

---

[1] Or, as many teenagers believe, a rather insidious form of torture.

research, and practice some more to learn just the right strategies and make just the right moves to achieve their goal. Goals motivate us in specific ways, pushing us to find the lessons we need to take, and helping us to extrapolate knowledge from the lessons we are forced to endure.

The future, for all of us, is in a constant state of flux. We all wake up every day and create it, decision by decision, action by action[2]. It is helpful to have a plan when we are making decisions and taking actions, and there is a good chance that plan will change. It is also likely that those plans will be swapped out entirely, sometimes by our choosing and sometimes not, forcing a complete reevaluation and restart. That is ok. That is life, which has an uncanny knack of reminding us that its only constant is change, just when we thought everything would stay the same. The fact that the average millionaire has been bankrupt more than three times in their life should be a lesson that how we respond to those often-unforeseen changes is what matters. Heroes on their journey know that the challenges will be many and severe at times, that they will be tempted to give up regularly, but they know that what they set out to achieve is worth it. What they set out for is their future.

There is danger in having no plan at all, primary of which is a lack of motivation to battle the dragons that stand in your way. Without the desire to reach a desirable destination, the first hint that effort will be required to move forward will be all it takes to halt a journey. While it may be true that not all who wander are lost, it is likely true that all those that are lost, do not have a plan. It's the rare kid that truly moves to their fixed purpose on iron rails, but developing a purpose, even a temporary one, and using that as a north star to guide the way and serve as the fuel necessary to keep moving forward is an important challenge teenagers will face in high school.

---

[2] This includes indecision by indecision, and inaction by inaction.

Groundhog Day

The 1993 movie *Groundhog Day* starring Bill Murray, who is one of my favorite people ever[3], is one of my favorite movies of all time. I remember at the time of its release seeing a commercial and learning of its premise, that a disgruntled TV weatherman gets trapped in Punxsutawney, Pennsylvania on Groundhog Day and experiences a time loop where he endlessly repeats February 2nd, Groundhog Day. To his dismay, he seems to be the only one aware of this time loop, and classic Bill Murray hijinks ensue as he deals with the folksy locals and attempts to break free and make it to February 3rd. After seeing the commercial I remember thinking to myself, "how far can they go with this premise?" Needless to say, being the Bill Murray fan that I was, and this being 1993, a time before Netflix when we actually went to theaters and watched movies with other people, some buddies and I went and saw it and had a great laugh. I remember being impressed with how they were able to take what seemed like twenty minutes of material and turn it into a complete movie. Bill Murray was hilarious as usual, and Andie MacDowell[4] was as beautiful and charming as ever. We were all entertained and believed our money was well spent. That was that. I was 23 years old at the time.

Many years later on a lazy weekend, I saw that *Groundhog Day* was playing on some cable station. In need of some horizontal couch time, I turned it on, planning to watch the first twenty minutes or so before relaxing into a pleasant afternoon nap. The nap never happened. I instead spent the entire time deeply engaged with the movie as if for the first time, remembering bits and details but understanding them completely anew, as if my brain were finally ready to interpret its true message. I was a fortysomething husband, father of two, and teacher that just watched one of the greatest philosophical deliberations on the meaning of life

---

[3] I have a painting of him hanging in my living room, next to one of Chevy Chase.

[4] A definite celebrity crush of my youth.

delivered by an American comedy icon, a large rodent, and a model turned actress.

Since that fortuitous click of the remote, *Groundhog Day* is the one movie I make sure to show my students every year. In early February, whatever we are doing, we take a break and learn about the importance of *tomorrow* by watching Bill Murray get (hilariously) stuck in today.

Tomorrow Gives Today Purpose

When Phil Connors, the weatherman played by Bill Murray that gets stuck repeating February 2nd over and over again, first learns of this bizarre and mystical twist his life has taken, he goes through the normal hysterics that anyone might upon learning they seem to have a severe case of deja vu that nobody else is experiencing. Once past this initial phase, Phil begins to settle into a life where tomorrow does not exist and there is only today. His first reaction? Great, no consequences!

He begins his new life of no tomorrows by indulging in whatever illicit scheme he can imagine, from car chases with the police, glutinous pastry binges, to bizarre role-playing dress up dates with a local woman. Each day is a new adventure to make the most of the day, knowing that whatever harmful or illegal activity he participates in, nothing will become of it. He will wake up tomorrow as if nothing ever happened and nobody remembers.

This eventually leads to a feeling of complete despair. He realizes that without tomorrow, today's actions are simply that, today's actions. They do not contribute to anything other than a moment of entertainment. They are the passing of time and nothing else. They do not contribute to anything *meaningful*. As a result, he becomes suicidal.

Phil attempts every method he can think of, from taking a toaster into the bathtub, to jumping off a tall building, to driving off a cliff with the groundhog in his lap, but they all fail. Each time he awakes as if nothing happened, doomed to repeat February 2nd.

Phil experiences a turning point when he attempts to save a homeless man that is dying. He tries without success many times to save a man whose time has come, but it begins a journey of personal development and giving that will eventually break Phil out of his loop. He begins by developing his skills, taking up the piano and ice sculpting to name a few, which instantly ignites a purpose in tomorrow: to build upon what he learned today. He also begins a commitment to service, and because he knows precisely when boys will fall out of trees, old ladies will experience flat tires, and restaurant goers will choke on meat, Phil is able to arrive just in time to save the day. Again, purpose in tomorrow is established by a need to help others.

Rita[5], who had denied his many attempted advances earlier by sensing the falseness of his motivation, notices a true change in Phil. Through all the universe's cruel tricks to strip Phil of his tomorrows, his purpose, he finds a way to reconstruct a reason to wake up in the morning and he is rewarded for his persistence. The movie ends on February 3rd.

The most successful students, like the most successful people, have a strong sense of tomorrow. They have a vision for what they want tomorrow to look like, and they are committed to the actions needed today to make tomorrow come to life. It is the foundation of a meaningful, purposeful life.

The least successful? Well, they are caught in a loop, eating donuts or binging YouTube videos. These activities bring momentary happiness, and as soon as they are done, the joy dissipates, and the urge to reach for another donut or click on another video kicks in.

What happens to these students?

Things Never Heard at High School Graduation

Every year in June at the high school where I teach, we gather at a neighboring school's football stadium for a huge, iconic life moment that none of us ever forget: high school graduation. The playing of *Pomp and*

---

[5] Played by the absolutely perfect Andie MacDowell.

Circumstance as the graduates file into the stadium and take their seats always makes me a little weepy. It is a special day for sure. There are some usually entertaining speeches from select students, an adult or two will give less than riveting orations, and then diplomas are dispensed, and caps thrown in the air. Afterwards, as graduates and family members mill around on the field, it is an opportunity to say goodbye to some of the students I have known since freshman year and have followed their journey to this night. When asked the question "if you could do high school all over again, what would you do differently?" some responses that have never left a graduate's lips include:

"I wish I had done less work."

"I would have not cared as much about my grades."

"I shouldn't have gotten so involved with activities."

"I wish I could go back, and ditch more, or at least racked up way more tardies."

"I should have gotten in more trouble."

"I probably would be better off with fewer friends."

"It'd be cool if people saw me as lazy and pathetic."

You get the picture (I hope).

The unfortunate truth is that nobody gets a high school do over, although many graduating seniors wish they did. Though the overwhelming mood of graduation is positive, there always exists an undercurrent of "*oh man, it's over and I have no idea what I'm doing and I don't have the skills or courage to tackle whatever life throws at me.*" Life gets real at that moment when young adults realize the safety and security of free, compulsory schooling has come to an end. All those caring, talented adults that monitored them, guided them, and challenged them are no longer at their service. In the eyes of our society, they are on their own. Hope they are ready!

This heavy moment causes many to reflect, for the first time, on how they have utilized this incredibly important and free service provided by our society. Those that have squandered this service, if they are honest with themselves, begin to wish for their do over. They start to imagine what they would do differently if a do over was granted.

"I wish I had done more work."

"I would have cared about my grades more."

"I wish I had played sports and gone to dances."

"I wish I had showed up every day on time."

"I should have stayed out of trouble."

"I probably should have been nicer to people and made more friends."

"It would be cool if people admired me for my work ethic."

Again, you get the picture (I hope).

When these graduating seniors look back at their imagined do over, they want to go back to day one of high school. They understand now how important the whole journey of high school is, and while it's not impossible to turn things around while you're in the middle of the journey, it sure impacts how far you get and how ready you are for what's next, adult life.

Goals & Vision

My father, before his passing, described to me his heaven. He was a man of faith, believing in a life beyond our time on earth, and he was not going to leave his final destination up to chance. He knew where he wanted to go, who was going to be there, and what it looked like. I was surprised a little, at first, by the pastoral country setting he described, one that involved horses and grassy meadows, coming from a man that grew up in suburban Southern California. But when he described getting to see his parents, his father having been raised in rural Oklahoma where he returned in retirement, and his mother having died young after suffering both physical and mental ailments, it made sense. This vision was, for him, beauty. It was a reconciliation, a making perfect of the previously imperfect. This was his ideal.

I had always understood the importance of vision, but it was this moment where I understood its power. Here was my father willing his afterlife into existence, one that I have zero doubt he is enjoying today.

It is extremely important that teenagers begin to develop a vision about their life after high school that excites them and that they accept as their own.

It is extremely important that teenagers begin to develop a vision about their life after high school that excites them and that they accept as their own.

That was not a mistake: it needed to be said again. We all know that the vision we have for our future, especially the ones we develop in our youth with the limited knowledge of how the world operates and what is possible, will likely change as we become more aware. That is ok. We need a vision to give us direction and motivation, because the life lived without one is directionless, and that is both sad and dangerous. It is Phil Connors endlessly repeating a day that never has a day after. It is empty. It is donuts and YouTube videos.

Goals and vision go hand in hand. The greatest leaders possess both in spades. The greatest bosses I have ever had were gifted at crafting and expressing a vision for our institution that everyone could clearly see and be inspired by. They were also great at articulating the goals that would serve as the bridge to that vision, the daily work needed to achieve our ends. The weakest bosses were good at supplying donuts.

Our children need to develop the skills of great leaders, because while they may never be called to lead other people, they will always lead their life. They will always be responsible for knowing where they are going, for deriving inspiration from that vision that will motivate them to do the hard work to get there, and for crafting the goals that will serve as the blueprint to achieve their desired future.

Talk about the future with your child. Encourage them to develop their powers of vision. Support but do not impose. This needs to be what they want.

Goals Lead to Pursuit, and That is What Matters

While many students, and all the best ones really, set specific grade goals (usually all As or all As and Bs), the attainment of the grade is the secondary benefit of the goal. While the grade itself is going on the transcripts, is contributing to their cumulative GPA (grade point average), all of which determine whether or not they get into the college of their choice, it's the skills developed in pursuit of that grade that will determine whether or not they complete college.

In the time since most of us went to college, the competition for college admission has increased significantly. Increasing the number of high school students applying for and being accepted into college has been a major focus of high schools for the better part of the last couple decades, and it is working. More and more students are completing the necessary courses in high school, and they are taking the necessary exams like the SAT and ACT. High schools are getting more students qualified, they are supporting more students in the application process, and more students are being accepted into colleges than ever before. American colleges are bursting at the seams with applications and newly enrolled students.

But because life likes to keep us on our toes, when we solve one problem, a new one presents itself. Our new problem? Students are dropping out of college at alarming rates.

If attainment of an A is the goal, then many things need to happen. Students must complete all the assignments on time and to a high quality. They must intensely train their focus during lectures and other times of information giving. Studying for tests is a must. Odds are, they are going to need to make a few sacrifices along the way. Managing time and maintaining organization are going to be vital allies in the desire to meet deadlines. Daily they will be required to effectively communicate, tolerate annoying classmates, forgive irrational teachers, recharge themselves with adequate sleep, keep themselves nourished with healthy food, and maintain hydration by drinking some water. In short, the attainment of a legitimate A requires that many things come together, and it's the development of those characteristics that will matter once they head off to college and have to complete much more challenging courses, *alone*.

Did you notice I snuck the word *legitimate* in there?

Like most things in life, there is the legitimate way of achieving or obtaining something, and there is the, uh, less than legitimate[6]. If a student sets out and earns an *honest* grade, the highest they were capable of, then their character was strengthened, and their skills and knowledge were developed. All future pursuits will become a little more attainable because of this sincere effort. This is the primary objective of school! Heroes do not become heroes by making it to the finish line; they are developed during the journey by overcoming challenges. It is the challenges that matter.

Can grades be earned less than honestly? You betcha, and in the age of technology, it is easier than ever.

The copying and dissemination of "the answers" to *anything* is so widespread it is overwhelming. While attempts can and continue to be made to get students to honestly complete their work, it is futile beyond the classroom, and even semi-futile within the classroom if technology is utilized in the work[7]. Every attempt to block students from taking shortcuts by blocking or restricting access to platforms or methods that make it possible, just leads to students finding a new shortcut, a new backdoor. I am going to stop here on this topic, before I get into full grandpa mode and start shaking my fist at those darned kids, because the solution most likely lies in the crafting of the vision.

When setting goals with your children, focus on the process, not the outcome.

When setting goals with your children, focus on the process, not the outcome.

---

[6] I was about to say illegitimate, and while many will truly cheat or cross the line into illegality in their pursuit of goals, I want to focus more on the taking of shortcuts here.

[7] Many high-income families are choosing to have their children educated using as little technology as possible. They understand, deeply, the skills necessary to achieve success, and they know how technology can stunt development of those skills, particularly deep thought and sustained focus.

Yeah, I did it again because it bears repeating. Goals, like "all As" or "4.0" can often lead to shortcuts. The reason for this is the outcome is what is sought, which opens the door to achieving those outcomes at any cost. This is not a reflection of whether the student is inherently good or bad...they are teenagers! With cell phones! And access to the internet! And pressure to perform! And pressure to qualify for college! I have witnessed too many supposedly "shocking" breaches of character from the supposedly straightest and narrowest of students to know one thing is certain: teenagers do stupid things.

Focusing on process goals will not eliminate the stupid, but it will frame their pursuit in a way that helps them to understand that it's the pursuit that matters, not the outcome. The beauty is, when the process goals are achieved, the outcomes are the ones everyone else was shooting for. The difference, however, is that those that focused on the process got there legitimately, while many of the outcome focused took shortcuts.

So, what specifically am I talking about? Instead of establishing goals that state a desired outcome, like "I want all As" or "I want to make the Honor Roll," help your child set goals that develop the habits that lead to those outcomes. Here are some examples:

- Complete all work on time
- Spend twenty minutes a day studying what I learned in (insert challenging course here) today instead of waiting for a test to cram
- Attend tutoring sessions X times a week for help with (insert challenging course(s) here)
- Read for thirty minutes a day
- Develop study groups with the best students in each class
- Communicate with my teachers at least once a week about my progress in class
- Go through my backpack and binder weekly to keep it organized

- Turn in work that reflects my best effort and my original thoughts and/or solutions
- Ask to be sat near the front of the classroom
- Keep a master assignment and test planner up to date
- Complete any work that is due tomorrow before (insert common work avoiding activity, like playing video games or going on social media, here)

I can keep going, but I think you get the picture. Can you see how a student that has some goals established like the ones above, can achieve outcomes similar to a student that has goals like "get all As" and "be on the Principal's Honor Roll," but be much better prepared to *complete* their college degree?

Goals and vision are vitally important to our children's future, but it is in the pursuit of that vision that matters. If their vision is going to materialize, help them craft goals, which serve as the bridge to their vision, that develop the strong habits that will see them beyond that vision. A well-constructed bridge, smartly engineered using quality materials, is the only bridge worth travelling on.

A bridge, made of shortcuts, is a risky venture.

Wrapping It Up

Delayed gratification is a concept lost on the unsuccessful. They do not get it, or more likely, refuse to get it. How dare we suggest that they put down the donut, close out of YouTube, and start doing work that will not pay off for a while. To them, school[8] is torture. In their mind, school was quite possibly developed by witches and ogres in the candle lit 1800s to enslave children and turn them into compliant servants.

Or they are just teenagers.

---

[8] School is a system that runs on delayed gratification.

The teenage brain is all about now, and donuts and YouTube are satisfying *now*. Developing the ability to craft a desired future and then map out the journey to get there, knowing that the journey will require difficult stretches and sacrifices, is an advanced skill. Without guidance and assistance from the caring adults in their life, two things will happen: they will not develop this skill and/or they will be wildly unrealistic in their vision.

Failure to develop this skill leads to endless pursuit of donuts and YouTube. It is a constant pursuit of the now and an ignorance of anything having to do with tomorrow. While Phil Connors experienced his time loop as a professional adult, with an adult brain and an adult's ability to reflect and think, a teenager ensnared in this situation is exactly that, a teenager. While their body will continue to develop, their character will remain stunted. I am sure anyone reading this can think of *biological* adults that are intellectually and emotionally, teenagers. They are impulsive, immature, and live solely for the now. They may also still live in their parents' house, be unemployed, and have massive credit card debt.

The wildly unrealistic are equally sad. Over the years, I have encountered so many young people that honestly believe that playing in the NBA is their future and they do not even play for the high school team. No, they did not get cut; they did not even try out! I have had an equal number becoming movie stars, who as I am sure you guessed, did not even audition for the school play. With the rise of online platforms, video gaming, and social media, the number of delusional future YouTubers, professional gamers, and social media influencers has hit an all-time high.

Sadly, these young people are always the least successful students. Their vision of the future is nothing more than a donut. It is a momentary boost that evaporates as soon as the last bite is digested. It does not lead to action. It does not provide motivation. It tastes sweet and that is about it.

Your child may very well make the NBA, become a movie star, or even a professional gamer. But they will not unless they vigorously develop the will to conquer the ten challenges. Success in any field requires many hours of hard work and dedication. It requires a vision and the ability to delay gratification. It also requires support. Keep in mind that teenagers and delayed gratification are not normally seen together in nature, so their struggle with it is not a deficiency: *it is normal.* Teenagers are ragingly present and all about *right now.* Working towards something in the future is a developed trait, one that will be derailed and fought against often by teenagers. It requires the part of the brain, the frontal lobe, that is responsible for self-regulation. In yet another example of nature's cruel sense of humor, this just happens to be the last part of the brain to fully develop, and this usually happens in the early twenties, or *after* high school. Take a deep breath or enjoy an evening beverage when moments that exemplify this lack of development occur. It is ok. Get them back on track tomorrow, and do not push too hard. Power struggles with teenagers never lead to the teenager happily and willingly doing what is in their best interest. It's in these moments of impasse, when both sides have begun to dig in, that if I take a moment to remember my teenage self in all of his goofy and irrational wonder, that my powers of empathy are finally able to engage and my temperature subsides. I can reset my objectives and remember that my role, as mentor, means I am not supposed to be driving. They are, and I am here to help them get *where they want to go.*

We, as parents and teachers of teenagers, need to engage in conversations with our children about their futures. It will evolve[9], it will be at times unrealistic, and it will be limited to what they know and understand about the world. After all, they cannot desire a future constructed of places, people, and pursuits they have not been exposed to or even know that they exist, right?

It is in these conversations that we are helping them develop a vision for their future, to really see it in their mind's eye. We are helping them

---

[9] Are you doing exactly what your teenage self thought you would be doing as an adult? Probably not. Only 1 in 4 college graduates end up in the field they earned their degree in. Additionally, most people do not find their occupational groove until they are in their late twenties or early thirties.

connect the actions they are taking now to the skills they are developing that will help them get there. We are also exposing them to more of the world, taking notice of their talents and interests and learning, together, fields of opportunity that they may not know exist.

The big picture goal for us as mentors is to help our teens get excited about their future, and to accept the notion of becoming an adult and the added responsibility of this next phase of life. The exact shape of their vision is not as important as is the mere *existence* of a vision. It is going to be a little messy, and it will probably be a little unrealistic, but a desired future creates passion in our children, and to watch your child pursue something with passion is incredibly satisfying. In that moment you know they are hooked. They are hooked on pursuing a life of passion, a life of their creation, a meaningful life that keeps them moving forward. They have taken ownership.

It is a life where you will no longer need to tell them to put down that donut or close out of YouTube. They will do it on their own. In that moment you know you have done your job.

They are an adult.

The Challenge's Impact on Trajectories

Ready for Take Off!

Leveraging all three phases of the life journey, the past, present, and future, these students move forward with purpose. Their past is constructed of enriching experiences, and their strong vision of the future ignites an extrasensory ability to recognize relevant activities in the present. They see opportunities that others miss, and they are willing to make sacrifices others are not. There is nothing timid in their journey, and while they are constantly moving into new territory, they are doing it with the confidence of someone that has studied and internalized the map. New roads seem familiar because they have thought about them for so long. Time is not wasted looking at the map, charting new courses, or being distracted by silly roadside attractions, so they get to their destination sooner. By beating the crowds, they experience less traffic and lower prices, and they are happy to take advantage of both. The assets they collect while out in front allow them to increase their lead. Their expertise with this challenge allows them to utilize this skill to achieve *anything*, and they do so again and again. While others continue to get lost without a vision, or struggle to craft an effective one, these adults are so good at the process they often have *too many* visions, excellent ideas bubbling to the surface in a constant stream. They simply abandon the unnecessary, share the important, and pursue the ones that light a fire in their soul.

Still Boarding

Our middle of the pack students have not quite mastered this challenge. They have the basic tools, but they have probably only been able to apply it to things they really enjoy, like sports or music, and these are most likely not their future. Once they learn how to translate this skill from something, they only use on activities they thoroughly enjoy, and train it on activities that will help them get ahead in the adult world, their journey will pick up steam. There's potential they do not do this, and instead spend their life pouring themselves into hobbies and sports memorabilia, assuming the "weekend warrior" approach to life. There is absolutely nothing wrong with this path, if their day job is not something they dread, and they end up hating Mondays and only living for the weekend. Life is too precious and short to swing wildly between days you cannot stand and days you cannot wait for. Developing a passion for a future beyond the coming weekend can help abate this.

Flight Delayed

Living a self-imposed Groundhog Day, these students are doomed to repeat the same day over and over. By refusing to develop a vision of a desired future, they pour all the energy into living in the moment or reliving the past. Because of this they are directionless, like a vehicle careening off the highway guide rails because the driver decided to take their hands off the wheel and engage in a card game with their passengers. Their life will likely resemble the vehicle in this scenario, more battered and worn than it should considering its age. Every day they wake up and begin to devour donuts and YouTube videos, and when they are done, they search for more. Nothing leads to anything, and because of it, each day is an endless search for instant gratification and momentary joy. To the passerby, it might appear this person is living a great life, constantly enthralled and always laughing. All it takes is twenty minutes of observation to find out otherwise.

PD for Parents & Teachers

For Parents

- Speak regularly about the future with your children. Share plans you have for something you want to accomplish or a skill you hope to develop. Ask them about their future. Make the future something real and something that is crafted. Make the future exciting and full of possibilities, and not scary and random. Talk about life after high school. What do they want to do, become, or accomplish? Be aware of their talents and expose them to careers they might enjoy but are not aware of. If possible, expose them to the people and places in the fields they want to go into. Make their future real for them, one where real people like them worked to achieve it.

- Have them imagine important moments, like graduation or when semester grade reports will arrive in the mail or be posted online. How do they want to feel when those moments happen? Connecting positive emotions to the future, a future earned through work done today, helps give today its purpose. Nobody ever wishes they could go back and do worse.

- When they achieve something, like good grades on a report card, praise and reward the work that went into it and not the results. Site specific moments, like the effort that went into a long project or the lunches they sacrificed to receive tutoring before the big test, in your praise. Place value in the vision and the dogged pursuit of that vision.

For Teachers

- Point out skills and accomplishments that took a while for your students to achieve. Highlight the work they put in and remind them of where they were when they started.

- When setting goals with students, have them focus on the process and not the outcome. Instead of "I want a 4.0," focus on processes like "Get everything done on time," or "attend lunch tutoring at least twice a week." These types of goals build habits that will be of benefit forever. Outcome goals are momentary and can lead to taking shortcuts to achieve.

- Get to know your students' goals and desires, and then connect the skills they are developing in school, like solving problems or meeting deadlines, to what they want to do after school. Help them find purpose in every class, regardless of subject, through the skills they are developing and how they will translate to post high school success.

Habits that Work for Teenagers

- **Every morning while I eat breakfast, I will envision myself successfully completing the major tasks I have that day.** Engaging in a little mental process simulation each morning helps the day be more successful. By mentally practicing challenging moments or conversations, and then envisioning their successful outcome, it feels as if the future is almost predetermined. The mental preparation also makes these moments rehearsed and prepared for, so when they encounter them it does not feel like the first time. They know what to do, and that gives them confidence.

- **Whenever I am out in the world, I will pay attention to different professions and imagine myself doing them.** This can be expanded to whenever they read or watch anything. By being curious about the extremely complex world of professions, students open their minds to what is possible. Most teens are only aware of professions held by those around them, and maybe a few others in the town they live in. If they live in a small town with limited industries, they might not connect with a future that excites them and matches their interests and skills.

- **At the end of each semester, I will reflect on my grades and how they were the results of the actions I took.** Developing the ability to delay gratification takes reflecting on accomplishments that took time to achieve. By appreciating the connection between an accomplishment and the work and sacrifice that went into it, students are better able to delay gratification in the pursuit of future goals.

Chapter Four

The Fourth Challenge:
MASTER the SYSTEM

Just because you don't understand it doesn't mean it isn't so.

From *The Blank Book* by Lemony Snicket

Most lawyers are handsomely compensated for their time, and rightfully so. They work long hours, have extensive education, and experience a lot of work-related stress. But so do I and many others, and we do not make nearly as much as lawyers do. So why do lawyers make significantly more than many other professions?

Lawyers have taken the time to master an incredibly complex system: the law. Forms and contracts are absurdly difficult to understand for most people, and there is great fear that the "fine print" exists to ensnare us. The courts are impossible to navigate, and their proceedings hold people's lives in the balance. Legal documents are required to get married *and* divorced. Buying a home, starting a business, and even going on a zipline adventure require that we acknowledge our rights and then sign them away. The law governs all aspects of our life, and it is not an easy and simple system. Lawyers' ability to translate, guide, and even manipulate an incredibly important system have earned them the right to charge high prices for their services.

While the law represents one of the most complex systems we will encounter in life, one that will often require the assistance of a well-paid guide, we will need to navigate most of life's systems on our own. Life is full of systems, and those that are skilled at learning and then efficiently moving through these systems will reap its greatest rewards. The rules and maps for these systems are rarely obvious or accessible. In fact, they were probably never committed to paper. The rules exist in the way that people move through them, and they become visible in the successes and failures those people experience. Systems learning requires acute powers of observation.

High school will be most teenagers' first opportunity to experience moving through a complex system with some level of independence and choice. There is the big system of classes and credits, where they will need to take and pass enough courses to earn a diploma. Some courses will be required, and others they will get to choose. Some they will take all four years, and others just one. Many courses will have different levels, from remedial to honors, and they will need to decide on a course by course basis which level makes the most sense for them and their goals. The big system of graduating high school supports many microsystems, with each class, club, and extracurricular activity deploying its own rules. Grading systems, teacher expectations, athletic try-outs, school transportation, ticket sales, and cafeteria procedures are just some of the microsystems teenagers will need to figure out to successfully make it to that graduation stage.

To do this, they need to seek guidance from trusted adults and peers, and they will need to closely observe how others move through the system, taking note of the consequences produced by their actions (or maybe inaction). These are the hallmark skills of those that become proficient at successfully getting the most out of all future systems, be it the workplace, stock market investing, local building codes, disability insurance, softball league politics, or social security. Knowing who you can trust, who to avoid, and closely observing and then emulating the actions of the most successful, will pay dividends, sometimes literally.

System mastery is dependent upon proficiency of the previous challenge, seeing the future. To get the most out of any system, high school included, it is important to know what comes *after it*. We want to be able to use each system as a springboard to the next one, gathering the assets our current system offers to help us do well in the next one. Students heading off to college after high school will need to make sure they take the right courses and tests and get the right grades and scores. They generally want to do the best they can, but different colleges have different requirements, and knowing those requirements can help guide their decisions. Is it better to get a B in an honors class, or an A in a regular class? Knowing where you are headed after high school will help you make those kinds of decisions.

This is a layered and pervasive challenge. Like epic tales that have potential heroes crossing an ocean that is infested with ship gobbling serpents, persuasive sirens calling from craggy outcroppings, and colossal swells generated by the gathering storm, successful navigation through this challenge will require gumption and keen mental agility. The bounty earned from this challenge, a set of magical keys that will unlock any door you choose to enter, is worth the effort.

A Beard Does Not Earn a Diploma

High school is a whole different ball game, and you need to understand the rules and how it is played, and quick.

The truth is every year a bunch of students make it to high school without really earning it. They got passed on not because their grades were good enough or because they learned a minimum amount of new stuff, but because it would be weird to have a six-foot-tall man child with a beard sitting in a 2nd grade classroom. To keep things from getting creepy, they get passed on.

We can get philosophical about whether this is right or wrong but let us save it for another book. For now, accept the system for what it is. We are here to help your teenager have the best four years of high school possible and knowing how it works is important.

Each school is different, but they regularly go through a process called "accreditation" where a bunch of smart people come and check to make sure they are doing a good enough job getting young people ready for college and life. If they are not, the diploma means nothing, and colleges will not accept their graduates. It is an important thing, and the schools really feel the pressure when going through accreditation[1], especially for the week the Accreditation Team is on campus. It is a huge sigh of relief when it is over, and the school learns that it received a positive report and the longest possible extension.

Part of being an "accredited" school is having a clear path to graduation, where students take certain required classes (classes like English, Science, etc.) and certain Electives (classes like Art, Auto Shop, etc.), earn passing grades in those classes[2], which in turn earns you credits towards graduation. Each school has a minimum number of credits you must earn to graduate, and if you do not get there, no diploma.

For example, where I teach, the students take 6 classes a semester, and earn 5 credits for each class they pass with a D or higher. If they pass them all, they earn 30 credits. By the time they graduate, they need to have earned 220 credits. For those doing the quick math in your head, yes 8 semesters of 30 credits would equal 240 total credits, not 220. Senior year is usually a little lighter and allows students to do things like Work Experience or Office Aide and free up some space to apply to colleges and have some fun before life grabs them by the collar and yanks them into adulthood kicking and screaming.

---

[1] Which happens every two to six years, depending on how strong or deficient the last report was.

[2] Which is a D or higher, and usually surprises students who thought it would be a C. Every year when I help my freshmen understand this, I ponder fudging the truth a little and telling them a C is required to pass, but I can never bring myself to do it.

At my school, like all others, those 220 credits cannot just be from classes they like. You cannot just take a bunch of PE and Auto Shop and expect a diploma. At my school, you need English all four years (40 credits), which is common. 30 credits of Science, and 30 more of Math, and so on. You get to make some choices, and you can often focus your electives in areas you enjoy, like Art or Technology. Many schools now have "Pathways" where students are grouped in cohorts around a common field, like Engineering, Business, or Medical. It is a cool development in education, and something you should explore with your kid to see if they are interested. Be on the lookout for any informational nights or videos your child's high school may share about any pathways they offer. There may even be a pathway at a neighboring high school that your child is interested in and seeking a transfer to enroll in a desired pathway is a common occurrence nowadays.

Students are going to have counselors that are hopefully great at helping them map out a course that gets them to graduation, while taking the right courses for the path they plan to take after high school. It is important that you and your student do not just rely on them to get your kid scheduled into the right courses. Take it upon yourself to learn how many classes and credits are needed, and regularly track the progress.

In the end, it is your child's diploma, and whether they earn one with their name on it depends on them earning enough credits.

Growing a beard is not enough.

Grades & GPA, a Refresher

Grades and GPA are at the heart of the school experience, and I am always so amazed at how little students and their parents understand them. I have thought that a standardized, national system of grades and grading would go a long way towards helping people understand what grades mean, how they are produced, and what they say about the student that earned them. That has absolutely no chance of happening in my lifetime, so I will stop wasting my breath and help you understand these very important records as best I can.

While your child may have experienced a somewhat recent trend in grading called "Standards Based Grades" or something like that in elementary and/or middle school, they are almost assured to encounter traditional grades in high school. The main reason for this is that high school transcripts, and the grades that appear on them, are the records used by students to apply to colleges, and colleges like traditional grades. In case you have forgotten, the traditional grades are:

A- Excellent
B- Above Average
C- Average
D- Below Average
F- Failing

As I stated previously, usually[3] grades of A, B, C, and D are sufficient for passing a class and earning credits towards graduation, while an F usually means no credits earned. The caveat here being that while a D is usually sufficient to earn credits towards high school graduation, many, maybe most colleges will not accept a grade of D as sufficient for credit in a college required course.

So, how are these grades determined? We'll get into more detail in the next section, but in general teachers require the students to do work in the form of assignments, like solving math problems, writing essays, reading a text and answering questions, or any of the myriad other ways teachers come up with to help their students understand a subject and develop skills. Work done to understand something, to build meaning, to practice new skills, is referred to as "formative" work. This is where

---

[3] I feel bad using words like "usually" and "many" instead of "always" and "all." The problem is that there is no standardization of systems between schools, school districts, counties, and states, or among colleges and universities. While everything I will tell you here is most likely true or close to it, you need to take it upon yourself to understand your child's system thoroughly.

the emphasis, usually, is on completion more than accuracy. This is the practice before the game.

The other broad category of work that gets factored into a student's grade is called "summative." This is what we usually refer to as assessment because this is where students are tested to see what they have learned. Summative work can take many forms, from traditional exams, to essays, to projects. In summative work, the focus shifts towards accuracy. We want to know what the student learned, and what they did not. This is the game, where the score matters.

Over the course of a grading period, usually a semester in high school (half of the school year), teachers collect the points students earned on all of their formative and summative work, enter it into a computer grading system[4], which produces a grade. These grades usually follow the traditional grading percentages:

A- 90-100%
B- 80-89%
C- 70-79%
D- 60-69%
F- 0-59%

At the end of a grading period, teachers produce grades for each student, and each students' grades are collected on a report that either gets mailed home through the mail or electronically, and most likely both methods. On this report, all the student's classes will be listed, and the final grade earned for the semester. There will also most likely appear the student's GPA, which stands for Grade Point Average. This value speaks to the student's overall competence in school, taking all subjects into account. While individual course grades will report a student's

---

[4] Which were just coming into broad use when I started teaching in 2000, before which grades were kept by hand and calculators were used to figure totals and percentages. It pains me to think of the millions of erroneously calculated grades that must have been produced prior to computer grading programs.

competence in that subject, GPA is an indication of their ability across the board. The higher the GPA, the more well-rounded the student.

GPA is calculated by assigning point values to the grades. They are as follows:

A- 4 points
B- 3 points
C- 2 points
D- 1 point
F- 0 points

To calculate the GPA, the grades earned for each class are translated to their point values, those points are added up, and then the total is divided by the number of classes. For example:

English- B (3 points)
Chemistry- A (4 points)
PE- A (4 points)
Intro to Foods- B (3 points)
Geometry- C (2 points)
World History- B (3 points)

Total Points (19) ÷ Number of Classes (6) = 3.16 GPA

Not to confuse you too much, but variations to how a GPA is calculated do exist. One of the main ones is that classes considered "Honors" or "Advanced Placement" will often earn an extra point because of the extra challenge[5], but you'll need to check with your school if they do that, and whether or not they do that for all four years. Freshman and Sophomore year honors courses can often not be awarded the extra point. Another variation is the calculation of both "Overall"

---

[5] For example, a B earned in Honors Algebra 2 could earn the student 4 points towards their GPA calculation.

and "Academic GPA," where one factors in all classes (overall), and the other removes non-academic courses like PE before calculating.

GPA is calculated for each grading period (again, usually a semester), and a GPA that represents ALL their grades in ALL their classes while in high school is also calculated at the end of each grading period. This is called the Cumulative GPA. At the end of a freshman's first semester, these two GPAs are the same[6], but afterwards you will start to see some separation as individual grading periods tick up or down, impacting their Cumulative GPA accordingly.

Understanding these terms, how they are calculated, and how they relate to and impact each other *at your student's school* should be one of the first things you and your teen figure out. It will impact some of the decisions you make together, and it will help you to better monitor progress and make the necessary adjustments in support.

How Teachers Grade: Do Not Ask Me

Grades are THE most important records that teachers produce, yet they receive very little or no attention in teacher credentialing programs. Also, in my experience, they receive very little or no attention from most district and school site administrators. By and large, teachers are allowed to produce their own systems for assigning point values to assignments and tests, for grading assignments, and for establishing their categories and their weights, which when you put this all together, produces a student's grade. Unless your child attends a high school that has addressed the issue of wildly disparate grading systems and policies that exist from teacher to teacher and subject to subject, they will attend a high school where each course they take is taught by a unique human being that has their own way of grading. Imagine a normal day of errands, where you run to the bank, then get your car washed, then stop by the grocery store to get a few things, and then finally head home. Now imagine that each time you got in your car, you were in a different

---

[6] Because their "cumulative" only consists of that one semester.

country, with different rules of the road, and you constantly had to adapt your driving to get to your next destination. Grading is kind of like that.

It is one of those "it is what it is" kind of situations. The bottom line is you and your student need to understand quickly how each of their teachers are going to produce grades. Each teacher is the commissioner AND referee of their own little league, and they are both going to establish and enforce the rules. Understanding those rules is paramount to successful completion of the course. While there may be great coordination or wild variation among the courses and their grading policies at your child's high school, there are a few things that any student can focus on to help them succeed in every class.

Now that we have computers to do the complex work of calculating grades, most teachers employ some system of weighted categories: Teachers establish categories, and every piece of work that receives points in a course will be attributed to one of these categories. Without weighting the categories (which may happen), this just organizes the assignments so that a teacher can see how a student is doing overall AND in any categories they have established. Most likely, your student's teachers will assign weights to the categories, and this is where the advanced student focuses. It is in the weighting where the teacher lets you know what they value, and this is of utmost importance. Remember, a teacher is the monarch of their kingdom, and your survival in the kingdom relies heavily on knowing what makes them happy. Knowing what they value is a big part of that.

Here's how weighting works. The teacher establishes their categories, and then they assign percentages to each category. The percentage represents the amount of the grade that will be determined by the work done in a category. Take for example these three examples that employ just two categories, Classwork/Homework and Assessments (these are very common categories):

Algebra
Classwork/Homework   20%
Assessments   80%

Biology
Classwork/Homework   50%
Assessments   50%

Auto Shop
Classwork/Homework   70%
Assessments   30%

So, how does this impact their final grade? Let us run a scenario through each of these systems to see how the final grade changes. Let us imagine a student, Ted, that is a diligent worker and gets almost everything done on time and to the standard established by the teacher. He is an average to above average test taker that would benefit from a little more concentration and studying. Ted earns the following percentage of points in each category as a result of his efforts:

Classwork/Homework- 95% (A)
Assessments- 79% (C+)

So, Ted is an A worker and a C+ test taker. When these are applied to the three classes, here are the grades that result:

Algebra
82.2% B-

Biology
87% B

Auto Shop
90.2% A-

Each course is using the same two categories, but how they weight them is very different. How they weight them tells you something about the course and what the teacher values. In algebra, subject mastery rules. Assessments, which in math are likely in the form of tests, determine the bulk of a student's grade. Studying for tests is going to be hugely important in this class. In Biology, the teacher values work and subject mastery equally. Students need to be balanced in this course, making sure they keep up with their work and prepare for assessments with equal vigor. In Auto Shop, work rules. Having a strong, workmanlike attitude is going to be important here, showing up every day to do whatever the teacher has assigned is going to be a valued trait in this class.

These are simple, but not uncommon examples. You may encounter teachers that go overboard in their categorization and produce something that looks like this:

Classwork   10%
Homework   10%
Quizzes   15%
Chapter Tests   25%
Participation   5%
Projects   20%
Benchmark   15%

If you get something that looks like this[7], do not get overwhelmed trying to figure it out. Instead, simplify it.

This teacher has broken apart classwork and homework, but together they equal 20%. They have also broken apart quizzes, chapter tests, and benchmarks, which are all assessments, but together they equal 55%. So far, exam preparation seems to be what this teacher values. The unknown at this point is projects, and whether this teacher uses projects as formative, a way to learn about something, where accuracy takes a back seat to effort and completion, or as summative, a way to assess knowledge of a subject or mastery of a skill, where accuracy and quality of product matter. If it is formative, we will lump it in with classwork

---

[7] Which in my opinion is unnecessary. The biology example is how I grade, simple and balanced, placing equal value on working and learning.

and homework, bringing their total to 40%. If it is summative, it goes with the other assessments categories to equal 75%.

By now you might be asking yourself, "don't I want my child to be good at everything? Don't I want my child to do all of their work *and* study for all of their tests?" Yes, you do. But the reality is that there are still only 24 hours in a day, and attention to any one class is competing for time with all of their other classes, along with any activities like sports or band that they may be involved in. The recent revolution in college and professional sports that prizes data analysis over old school scouting[8], has helped people understand that not everything matters equally. Some things matter more to the outcome than others and knowing this allows us to focus our efforts where it matters, especially when time and or resources are stretched. Being able to effectively prioritize is an important skill and knowing each teacher's grading system allows students to do just that.

Master the Semester

If you ever watch kids run a race that's a quarter mile (1 lap around the track) or longer, it's easy to tell those that have been trained how to run distance and those that haven't. The untrained do not know how to pace themselves. They do not know the crucial segments of the race, the times when they need to conserve energy or pour it on. The untrained start at a sprint, tire quickly, walk, sprint a little more, tire even quicker, walk a lot more, and eventually finish well behind the true runners. They had no concept of the race's length or how to manage their resources to most effectively keep pace with the demands of the race. They had it in them to run the entire race and finish with a good time, they just did not know how.

Conversely, watching an Olympic swimmer or runner, especially in the early qualifying rounds is watching a work of art. The better Olympic

---

[8] This shift was documented in the fantastic book *Moneyball* by Michael Lewis, which was made into a great movie starring Brad Pitt.

swimmers and runners know how to go out and get a specific time, the time needed to advance them to the next round. They know exactly how to pace themselves, when and how to breathe, and exactly how many strokes or strides it takes them to get them through the lap. They are masters at prioritizing their resources, assessing the conditions around them, conserving energy when they can, and channeling their focus and power at just the right moment. Michael Phelps, one of the greatest Olympians of all time, famously had his goggles fill with water as he dove in for the start of the 200 butterfly in the championship heat at the 2008 Olympics in Beijing, China. Phelps, however, was so prepared for this race, his signature event, that he was able to do it blind. He knew exactly how many strokes it took him to get to the wall, allowing him to take home another gold medal.

The semester is a race, a long race. Students need to know how to swim it, even if their goggles fill with water.

A strong start is essential. The start of the semester, especially the Fall or first semester, is when a lot of important information is dispersed, rules and policies are established, and the first assignments are given. Being present and alert, asking questions, and getting a good sense of the teacher's expectations and what they value is extremely important. Waiting until later, through trial and error, to understand how a class and teacher operates is not a good idea. It would be like playing a game of basketball without knowing the rules, instead waiting for fouls and rules violations to be called against you to learn how to play. By the time you picked it up, the score would be so lopsided you would have no chance to catch up. Also, the first assignments in a semester are usually on the easier side, covering introductory material. It is crucial that students gobble up as many easy points as possible. Run up the score when the defense is sleeping. Eventually the assignments are going to get tougher and having as large a cushion of points as possible will help soften any lapses that may occur.

The middle of the semester usually kicks in when the first major test or other assessment is levied, like for a chapter or unit, and continues until right before finals or benchmarks are given. In chess this is called the middlegame, and it is here where most matches are won or lost. In the middlegame, each chess player is looking to gain a material advantage, trying to keep as many of their pieces while eliminating as many of their opponent's pieces as possible. The idea is to head into the endgame with the strongest army possible. In the grueling middle of a semester, which could be fifteen weeks in length, maintaining good habits like not missing any assignments, accessing tutoring prior to exams, and taking advantage of all opportunities for extra credit or easy points is key. Students want to move into the final leg of a semester in a position to finish strong. Again, stuffing the gradebook with as many points as possible heading into finals is a desired position. It relieves stress knowing that if they are not at their best, they can fall a little and still be alright. This reduced stress usually turns into better results. It is like a team that heads into the fourth quarter with a big lead, knowing they can afford to give up a few big plays and still walk out with a victory. Oftentimes, because they are playing so loose and confidently, while the other team is stressed and trying too hard to make up a deficit, the team with the lead increases it by capitalizing on their opponent's mistakes.

The final stretch, the endgame, is the shortest period of the semester. It is just the last week or two where final assessments are given. It might also include some review time in preparation for the final exam. It is now the end of the semester, and everyone is abuzz about the upcoming winter or summer break, but somehow students need to be able to focus and have their best performance of the year. This is the Super Bowl, and while the streets are full of fans and revelers, and every news outlet in the world has cameras trained on the athletes, they need to find a way to tune it all out and focus on the task at hand: performing at their highest level possible. This is where healthy routines really pay off. Regular sleep, healthy meals, and periodic rest and exercise will enable students to be at their physical and mental peak. Ultimately, however, this is going to come down to whether they know their stuff. If they have had a strong semester to this point, odds are they do. But they should not see a good semester to this point as an excuse to undertrain. If anything, this is when they need to train their hardest. It is just a week or two, and some sacrifices need to be made. A little less phone time, and a little more study time will go a long way. Remind them that a big break is around the corner, when the alarms get turned off and some late-night phone binges will be allowed. But those moments will only be truly, deeply enjoyable if they are coupled with a report card, that is held by magnets on the fridge, that reveals the best outcomes that were possible.

Fall vs Spring

One of the great aspects of volleyball is that the winner is not the team that scored the most cumulative points, it's the team that scored the most points in three out of five possible games, or two out of three for younger programs. A team could get destroyed in two games, but if they can squeak out victories in the other three, they win the match. Unlike sports like baseball, soccer, basketball, or football, where the score carries over from inning, to half, to period, to quarter, volleyball resets to 0-0 after each game. No matter how poorly, or conversely how well you played in the previous game, there is no hole to climb out of or hill to rest on. Each game is a fresh start, and you will need to prove yourself all over again.

Semesters in high school are similar. Each one is its own, self-contained unit. Anything you did in a previous semester does not factor into the grade you will receive in the current one. Likewise, whatever the outcome is in the current semester, it will not impact your grade in future semesters. Each semester is a fresh start, and while what you did or did not learn previously will influence your performance in any given semester, as far as grades are concerned, they always get reset to zero.

While the two semesters that comprise a school year would appear to be identical units that require the same effort, they have some subtle differences that cause many students to experience imbalanced performance from one semester to the next. That imbalance is usually one of declining performance in the spring as compared to the fall.

You might think that students improve as the year goes on and they become more accustomed to the rhythms of each course, the expectations of each teacher, and any nervousness they may have at the beginning has long since dissipated. While this may be true for some, I have seen the opposite happen way too often.

The Fall Semester has a few things going for it that usually cause performance to be higher. First and foremost, students are never as focused, quiet, and attentive as they are at the start of the school year. Freshmen are nervous and totally compliant, not wanting to step out of line or receive any negative attention. They do everything you ask them to when the school year begins in the fall. They do every assignment, stuffing their grades with points which will buoy their grades as they start to fade towards the end of their first semester. Also, the first semester starts slowly. The beginning of the year includes a lot of time spent establishing rules and policies, doing paperwork, dispersing textbooks and devices, getting PE clothes and lockers, and participating in classroom level community building. In most classes, launching into the curriculum of the subject takes a while, which makes this semester a little lighter from a workload perspective. These two aspects of the Fall Semester, heightened attention and compliance along with lighter workload, often lead to slightly inflated grades.

When the Spring Semester kicks off, teachers head straight into the work. Students, many of whom had faded during the fall but ended with decent grades, fail to acknowledge that those grades were inflated by their burst at the start of the year. It is like a kid that starts the mile by running the first lap, maybe even the first lap and half, but then starts walking before they have finished two laps, or the halfway point. Upon hearing their time at a half mile while walking, they erroneously believe that they can continue walking and their second half time will reflect their first half time. They forget all the running they did! An increase in workload coupled with declining effort often leads to students receiving poorer grades and lower GPAs in their Spring Semester. In some areas, the Spring Semester may even be longer by a week or two than the Fall

Semester, which only compounds the previously stated extra challenges of this semester.

Another aspect of the Spring Semester that can make it more challenging, that while the gradebook was reset to 0, most of the material covered will in some way relate to or build upon work done in the fall. Math, probably more than any other subject, relies on mastery of previously learned material to be successful with new concepts. For this reason, while the spring may and should be viewed as a fresh start for a student that did poorly in the fall, this is a tough task considering the spring's reliance on what was learned previously.

Ultimately, we want our young people to be successful each semester, but life happens and sometimes we underperform. We do not throw in the towel, we do not lower expectations, and we do not dwell on it. Ideally, we learn from it and do better next time. If students can learn how to master the start, middle, and end of a semester, and combine that with knowledge of the subtle differences of the spring and fall to adjust accordingly, then they will start to string together successful school years.

That is a trajectory—consistently strong performances—any teacher or parent can feel good about, because it leads to a stable, successful adulthood.

Wrapping It Up

I recently purchased a computer and had a young man just a year or two removed from high school help me with the purchase. We got to talking about high school and I asked him if he was involved in any activities. He said he played football and had played it since he was a young kid. We talked a little about local high school football, and then he volunteered that while he loved playing, he never really understood the rules. Offsides, when a defender crosses the line of scrimmage prior to the offense hiking the ball, one of the simplest rules to observe and understand, just escaped him. He never got it.

We moved onto other topics and I completed the purchase, but I could not stop thinking about a boy playing football from youth leagues through high school, and never picking up on the most basic rules. How lost he must have felt! Or maybe he was not lost at all. Maybe he was blissfully ignorant of the mistakes he was making or the lack of progress he was making. Maybe he was just happy to be with his friends, running around, tackling opponents, and pouring Gatorade on the coach. Maybe, but, really?

Success in any field requires an intricate knowledge of the system within which you are working. Knowing the basics is only the start, but the truly successful love to dig deep into the nuances of how something operates in order to not miss an opportunity, to most effectively deploy their resources, and to not waste their time following nonsense down the rabbit hole. They take the time to get to know the people that wield the most power, or better yet, that will wield the most power over them. They want to know who the gatekeepers are, and what it takes to get them to open. They not only want to know the rules, they read the fine print to understand the loopholes and obscure policies that can be accessed to their advantage. They do not waste their time on actions that do not move them forward, and they double down on those moves that have the greatest returns. While some are getting spit out of the system because they rebel against the rules and the rulers, and others find themselves lost in the maze of meaningless tasks and red herrings, those that emerge at the top took the time to learn the map before proceeding. They always knew where they were going.

Life is one big system made up of a million more. Learning how to effectively learn and operate within them is a crucial skill, one that will propel, or delay, your child's progress. As Dan Heath astutely points out in his enlightening book *Upstream: The Quest to Solve Problems Before They Happen*, "every system is perfectly designed to get the results it gets." He later warns that "if you can't systematically solve problems, it dooms you to stay in an endless cycle of reaction." While this challenge is designed to develop a teenager's skill of systems analysis, these quotes point to a very important future skill that evolves from mastery of this challenge: systems architecture. Our goal is to be able to construct systems that produce the life results we desire. But first, our teens must learn to observe, evaluate, and then master the ones that exist on their journey.

The Challenge's Impact on Trajectories

Ready for Take Off!

These students, having successfully navigated the high school system because they realized quickly that *it was a system*, are transferring those skills into every new situation they encounter. They take the time to study as much as they can before entering, and once they do enter, they step back and take in the whole scene. They do not rush in, instead knowing that a little time spent watching the interplay of the moving parts is crucial before making their first move. Choosing the most effective and efficient entry point can make all the difference in the outcome. While others get caught in endless loops or get stuck in long lines that never seem to move, these students zoom past in the carpool lane, arriving at their destination well before anyone else. Their promotions happen faster, and their investments grow larger. Their knowledge of systems makes them a sought-out resource, and this creates yet another point of leverage that they utilize for advancement. They also become effective at creating systems that produce favorable outcomes, both personally and for any groups they are involved with.

Still Boarding

While these students understand that systems exist, they are a little clunky when it comes to navigating them. They sometimes do not do enough homework prior to entering, which can lead to delays, like someone that does not check their phone before hopping on the freeway and gets stuck in accident traffic. Had they checked, they could have taken the alternate route and been to work on time. They make it through systems, but it might take a little longer, and they may get a little less out of it than their more effective peers. While they may never become a master of all systems, they may master a few that they spend a lot of time in, or those systems they really enjoy. Hopefully, these systems are positioned to provide them with great satisfaction and fulfillment, like at work. Or maybe they provide them an opportunity to be an expert, someone qualified to give advice and help others.

Flight Delayed

It is likely these students do not understand or believe that systems exist. They fail to comprehend the intricate arrangements of wheels, gears, and levers, and instead believe everything is independent and not related. This leads to constant confusion, anger even, at why things are happening the way they are, unable to see how their actions set them off. To them, the world is random and chaotic and unfair. They play the lottery because they believe that's how people get ahead in the world, by luck. Their lack of system knowledge means they get frustrated easily, especially when trying to navigate more complex systems that involve more steps. This frustration often leads to a withdrawal altogether, choosing instead to stick with simpler, two and three step systems that they can handle: buy a lottery ticket, read the winning numbers in the newspaper, throw lottery ticket away.

PD for Parents & Teachers

For Parents

- Find out the graduation requirements for your child's high school and meet with a counselor to map out the four years of courses they will take, making sure to account for advanced requirements desired colleges or universities may have. Then meet yearly to update the plan, as course offerings may change, and your child's interest may change as well.

- At the start of each school year, sit down with your child and look at the class syllabi they have collected. Take the time to learn each teachers' grading policies. Find out where each teacher places value and discuss a strategy to meet that teacher's expectations. You know that coworker that seems to move up the ladder quickly, earning raises and promotion faster than others? They are very skilled at this: learning what their boss values and then making them happy by exemplifying that value. Developing this skill will add great value to your child's future.

- Be continually interested in how your child's school operates. Engage in low stakes conversations with your child about different aspects of the school, and in doing so you are modeling a practice of being observant of the systems we find ourselves in. Most teenagers rarely train their view beyond three feet of their navel, so opening their eyes to the world beyond will take effort. But it will be worth it, as advancement in life is going to take observing, understanding, and then efficiently moving through many systems.

For Teachers

- You are a system master! Help your students understand how to best navigate the often-confusing maze of requirements that is high school, especially if you work with freshmen. Make announcements and post information about things like courses that might require applications, informational events planned to help students and parents better understand programs or tests and how to register for them, and opportunities to get involved with extracurricular activities like sports and drama.

- Make sure your grading system is simple, clear, and fair. Take the time to explain it, at length, with your students so that they have a firm grasp of your expectations and policies, and how their grade will be calculated. Have easy to follow workflow systems and be consistent and timely in your grading.
- Be a tour guide through the semester. Instead of just heading off on a walk and hoping that your students all follow along, take the time to stop and point out details. Help them to find a good pace and avoid common pitfalls. Help them start and end strong, and redirect those that have strayed from the pack. They are going to get better at pacing themselves through the semester if they get taught how.

Habits that Work for Teenagers

- **If I am not sure how a score was earned on an assignment, I will ask the teacher.** Seeking clarification is good practice, because it helps to make sense of how the system works and how the next attempt can be improved. But it also establishes a good practice of engaging with experts in the field, a strategy they can begin to use preemptively before they even make their first attempt.
- **When I am walking around campus, I will read any posters and flyers I see.** Understanding systems means being observant and scanning your environment, making sure opportunities are not missed. Schools are often large and unwieldy places, and their communications systems are not always the most efficient. Sitting back and waiting for information to find its way to you is a bad idea in any system. Having your eyes and ears open and alert is a much better practice.
- **Whenever extra credit is offered, I will do it.** The best students do extra credit assignments, even when they have a 100% in the class. They know that 105% is better. Lazy students

wait until they have an F, and then they desperately need extra credit to keep from failing. Taking advantage of all opportunities for extra credit is a successful mindset, just like picking up extra shifts in August to keep from having to use credit cards to pay for Christmas is.

Chapter Five

The Fifth Challenge:
EMBRACE CRITICISM

People ask you for criticism, but they only want praise.

From *Of Human Bondage* by William Somerset Maugham

For many, this will be the greatest challenge of all because it feels personal. It can stir the emotions, especially the uncomfortable ones like fear and embarrassment. This challenge, more than any other, can feel like an attack.

"I'm being picked on," and "The teacher doesn't like me," are common utterances from students that struggle with this challenge.

Norman Vincent Peale, the minister and author of *The Power of Positive Thinking* once said, "The trouble with most of us is that we'd rather be ruined by praise than saved by criticism." It is hard to imagine that the guy who wrote a book about *positive thinking* was in favor of criticism, but he wrote that book in 1952. Our relationship with criticism was very different then. Our skin has thinned a bit in the decades since.

Unfortunately, the world we find ourselves in today has made it difficult for criticism to find open ears and minds. Between the deluge of unearned and overblown praise heaped upon our children in sports leagues and schools—where everyone gets a certificate and corrective feedback cannot be given if not sandwiched between thick slices of praise—and a virtual world of trolls and haters spewing vile insults from the cowardly veil of a username, criticism is itself under assault. Even in an exploding online economy where reviews are an integral part of the buying experience, it is difficult to tell the genuine from the manipulative.

Criticism is everywhere in high school, and the challenge for your student will be to embrace it. They will need to discern between criticism meant to make them better (*constructive* criticism), and criticism meant to hurt. I would like to say that good criticism will come from the adults and bad from their peers, but the world is not so perfectly organized[1]. Emotions are going to get roused and feelings bruised as criticism is personal, and hurtful criticism grotesquely so. It is difficult for young people (all people really) to separate criticism of their product from criticism of themselves. Tuning out words meant to hurt and focusing on those meant to improve, all the while leading with the head instead of the heart will be crucial. There is a persistent riddle embedded within this challenge, requiring the hero to fine tune their listening and critical thinking skills. To help them solve the riddle, they will constantly be asking themselves questions like: *What should I listen to? Who should I listen to? How do I interpret that? How do I apply that? Should I ignore that?*

How they write, speak, solve, recall, interact, and create will all be scrutinized, picked over, and offered suggestions for improvement. "That's perfect" is a phrase they should not get used to hearing and, if they do hear it, they should be leery. Embracing criticism is an incredibly advanced skill: one many never master. It is probably the most difficult of the ten challenges, but it also has the most potential for great, positive life improvements if mastered.

The more they are involved in, the more criticism they will receive. Play basketball and the coach is going to critique their shooting technique, and there will be plenty of data to back it up. Play in the band, and the director's criticism will determine whether your child is first chair

---

[1] Hence the need for the challenges—to prepare youth for a complex and unpredictable world.

or further down the row. Serve on the prom committee, and every attendee is going to offer their criticism. Join the yearbook staff, and the adviser is going to critique your student's layout and photo selection. *Every* application submitted for *anything*, where the feedback will be *acceptance* or *denial*, will be a critique of their record and their ability.

Because embracing criticism is such a mature task, one that requires deft management of internal states, this is a challenge that few will master, and many will continue to struggle with well into adulthood. At the high end of the spectrum we have a smallish group that fully accepts and masters the challenge, effectively embracing criticism to improve their skills and performance. Unfortunately, at the other end we tend to see a heartbreaking number that fail miserably, discounting any criticism as a personal attack and avoiding any extra activities because of their inherent critical nature. In the middle, we have a large group of partial completers, those that struggle to effectively determine whether feedback is helpful or hurtful, often relying on personal relationships instead of the message itself.

Step on the Scale

When scientists have studied people that are good at managing their weight and staying healthy, they discovered something they have in common: they have a scale that measures their weight, and they step on it every morning.

This might seem excessive to you. *Daily? Really? How much can change in a day?* You are right to think that because not a whole lot can change in a day.

But these people, the ones that are good at managing their weight, which is a really BIG factor in living a long, healthy life, are not waiting for large, noticeable changes. They want to know if there have been *any* changes since yesterday.

They are seeking constant, regular feedback on whether their actions— what they are eating, how they are exercising—are having the impact they desire. If they are trying to lose weight, they want to see it. If they are trying to stay put or even gain weight, they want to see that too. They want to know how their actions are working, and they are making decisions based on that information. They are not waiting until it is too late. They want to know about any change, fractions of a pound kind of change, and they want to know now.

What they are doing is either working or not, and they are not afraid to know which one that is. Their goal is too important to them to ignore the truth.

Life has many scales to check how you are doing, and you are either going to use these scales, or you are going to avoid them. In my experience, people that ignore life's scales, experience more of life's struggles.

A student's scale is whatever online grading system their school uses. I would be surprised if there was a school out there not utilizing an online system to input and calculate grades that both students and parents can access today. It is one of the better technological advances that is positively impacting student outcomes[2].

Students must step on this scale daily. To ignore it is foolish.

If something is missing, they need to know. If a teacher made a mistake on a score, they need to catch it and get it corrected. If their grade is or is not what they want it to be, they want to know. They want to know whether what they are doing is translating into the grades they desire, and they want to adjust their academic behaviors accordingly.

Or, they can ignore it, like the binge shopper ignores their online banking account information right before they receive an eviction notice.

Avoid the Sinkholes

Every so often a traffic camera captures a harrowing sight, as an unsuspecting driver falls victim to a massive hole that miraculously

---

[2] I do not feel that way about most educational technology, but that is for another book.

appears where previously there was a seemingly stable stretch of road. Within seconds, a driver that was just attempting to get to the store and grab some milk for tomorrow's breakfast, finds themself nose first in the muddy earth ten feet below where they were a moment ago, and ten feet below where they'd rather be now. It is as if the earth got hungry and decided to gobble up the Toyota and its driver that were just heading to the store, minding their own business. What a horrifying experience for the driver!

Usually what happens in these cases is some kind of water, maybe from excessive rain or a broken pipe, has caused the ground deep below the surface to erode while the top layer stays intact, eventually giving way to something heavy like an unsuspecting Toyota. They seem to appear out of nowhere, without any warning, wreaking havoc on those unfortunate to fall victim to their surprise appearance.

I have seen too many students, particularly those that fail to *step on the scale* on a regular basis (daily is best, weekly at minimum), experience similar fates as the Toyota. Only these sinkholes appear in their grade or grades, not the earth.

Missing assignments are like a broken pipe spewing water under the road. If the pipes are inspected regularly, the break can be addressed, the pipe repaired, and the ground beneath the road reinforced to allow those driving above to continue to do so safely. Fail to inspect the pipes, and there goes the Toyota.

Missing assignments happen for many reasons—laziness, illness, school activities or field trips to name a few. There are going to be instances when a student misses out on school work, either by choice or circumstance, and if they don't check into their grading system and do the work or ask for the help necessary to get caught up, the missing work can pile up. Before they know it, a giant hole in their grade opens and they are ten feet deep with an F and a lot of work to do to get themselves out of it.

There is an unfortunate phrase that people often succumb to uttering when they find themselves in this situation.

Never, Ever Say "What the Hell"

The "what the hell" effect is a real thing. I did not make it up. Scientists did. I am not kidding.

Scientists were studying people in certain situations, particularly when they were trying to achieve something, like losing weight on a diet or saving money towards a big purchase like a car. Because these are long-term goals that take longer periods of time and lots of discipline to achieve, the likelihood that there are going to be some bumps in the road are highly likely, almost inevitable. What they found happening when people encountered these bumps, like breaking their diet by having some cake at a party or not being able to save money one month because of an unexpected expense, some people were saying "what the hell" and abandoning their goals. They went back to their poor eating and spending habits and gave up on their goals. All it took was one mistake to unravel everything.

Grade sinkholes can have this effect on students. I have never had a student start the semester saying, "I want a D" or "I'm ok with failing and taking this class again in the summer." Even in the rarest cases do students set a goal of earning a C. Most students start every semester wanting an A or B in every class.

I firmly believe, in high school, an A or B is attainable by *almost*[3] every student in *almost* every class. It is not easy, and it should not be, but if the right combination of effort and attention are applied, it is possible. I firmly believe that, and nobody can convince me otherwise. Most students know it too, and that is why it is a common goal when the semester starts. "I want all As and Bs" is the most common goal related to grades, and while I encourage the crafting of goals that focus on processes like "getting all homework done on time" that help lead to those outcomes, the point remains that all students start each semester

---

[3] I use "almost" here to leave wiggle room for those students that may have greater than normal obstacles to success and have accepted a challenge greater than maybe they should have. In these cases, a C is seen as a victory.

wanting to achieve the highest they are capable of. It is human nature to want to do well.

But like losing weight or saving up for a car, a semester grade is a long-term goal, and there will be bumps: miss a week because of an illness, drama from a break-up, basketball practice and games every day after school. Being able to navigate these bumps is part of high school, and a necessary part because life is not smooth, and we need to be ready. And be alert to any potential sinkholes.

Students are going to be challenged, and a part of them, the part that wants to take it easy and watch some more Netflix or play more video games, will tempt them to say "what the hell." Do not give in! "What the hell" is the death of As and Bs, and it's a short distance to "I didn't really want to go to college."

Seek the "Mean" Teacher

Ms. Sebastian was cold. A tough as nails, never smiling, ex-military ice queen. At least that is what my high school self thought, and buddies I had that were older had warned me as such. When I picked up my schedule the summer before my sophomore year and saw that I got placed in her Social Studies class, my heart sank. *Crap*[4]! My year, I thought, was going to suck.

I probably grew more that year, in that one class, than under any other teacher I ever had (but you probably saw that coming).

I would learn much later that Ms. Sebastian was what is referred to as a "warm demander," the most effective teaching type there is. She cared to build relationships with her students (warm), and she had high expectations for their performance and growth (demander).

There are those that are caring without expectations. These are the easy pushovers that students tend to think are "cool." Some teachers have ridiculous expectations paired with a cold, bordering on dickish personality. These teachers deserve whatever vile graffiti appears on their

---

[4] Actual word or phrase was most likely more colorful.

desks. There are still others, the burnouts that radiate nothing, neither care nor expectations. These are the ones that give teaching tenure its abhorrent reputation.

Ms. Sebastian hit the sweet spot. Teenagers are not naturally inclined to have expectations hoisted upon them, and teachers that do can be unfairly labeled as "mean" by students that just want to chill and watch movies. The warm demanders would never let a day be wasted in such a fashion. They will be prepared, every day, with meaningful work that they expect their students to do and to a standard just beyond what they think is reasonable. They want to stretch their students. They understand that each student is somebody's child, somebody's universe, and they take that seriously. They also know that each student represents a future neighbor, a future nurse, a future congressman. Each student, to them, is more than a single life. It is the future of the world. Ms. Sebastian, who had served her country in the military, brought that same commitment to the classroom. She saw everyday as a battle to save the world through her work with us, her students, and chilling with a movie was not going to cut it.

In David Epstein's compelling 2019 book *Range: Why Generalists Triumph in a Specialized World*, he highlights how effectiveness and likeability do not always go hand in hand, at least instantly, when it comes to teachers. He cites a study done with Calculus 1 professors at the Air Force Academy, where student performance on the Calculus 1 final exam, their evaluations of their Calculus 1 professors, and their performance in subsequent courses that required application of Calculus 1 knowledge were all compared. It is not surprising that students that performed better on the Calculus 1 exam also gave their professors high marks on the end of course evaluations. Those professors helped them succeed *now*, those students felt good *now*, and they rewarded their professors with positive evaluations. It is also easy to understand how students that struggled more with the exam, were more likely to rate their professors more critically. Professors' ratings and students' performance in their classes were linked: higher performances received higher ratings; lower performances received lower ratings.

But here is where it got interesting. When researchers looked at the next set of data, how those students performed in courses that required them to apply what they learned in Calculus 1, the relationship between Calculus 1 professor rating and performance in subsequent courses where that knowledge was applied was inverted: the lower the professor rating, the better the student did. *Why?* As it turns out, those professors that were more challenging, that created a feeling of discomfort in their students by pushing them to think more deeply, were not simply doing so because they were "mean." They understood that to develop better long-term understanding, some short-term gains needed to be sacrificed, and that does not always feel good. Hence the less than stellar reviews by students that did not feel immediately satisfied. And let us not forget, these were *Air Force Academy cadets*, not high school teenagers! Even very mature and driven young adults can have distorted assumptions of teacher effectiveness based on how they feel and perform *now*.

Many of us have those people in our lives, mentors of some capacity, that we did not really care for in the moment but come to appreciate much later. I was a typical teenager not stoked about spending a year under the thumb of that icicle, Ms. Sebastian. I can say, confidently, that I would be something less today had I not.

Wrapping It Up

The fifth challenge, embrace criticism, requires teenagers to listen to other people tell them "you suck." They will not actually say that, but that's how teens tend to interpret it. Our job, as parents and teachers of teenagers, is to get them to hear something different. So much of life is how we interpret the explicit and implicit messages we receive. When a teacher provides feedback on how to better craft a thesis statement for a student's persuasive essay, the student that interprets it as "you suck at writing thesis statements" will wilt, while the student that hears "I know a way to turn your average paper into something great," will flourish. Perception of the message is key.

The Fifth Challenge: EMBRACE CRITICISM

Everywhere you look in the world, there are richly successful people that appear, from the outside, to no longer need feedback. They have reached the top of their profession and can afford to hit cruise control. But instead, what you see are voracious consumers of criticism. Professional athletes, who already receive massive amounts of criticism from their team's coaching staff, hiring trainers and dieticians to critique their routines and give them that boost needed to go from reserve to starter, or from starter to all-star. The CEO that hires an outside consultant to come into their company with fresh eyes and advise ways they can improve their company culture. Elected officials that assemble a "team of rivals" because they want to effectively serve everyone, and hearing dissenting voices is crucial to crafting caring policies.

The moment we stop listening to critiques of our performance is the moment our trajectory stalls. Whether it flatlines or begins to crash will be determined by many factors, but an upward path is no longer possible. For an upward trajectory, embracing criticism is the jet fuel that makes it possible.

The Challenge's Impact on Trajectories

Ready for Take Off!

This student learns to not take criticism personally, and as a result is able to embrace it. Once they do, they start to separate from the rest of the pack. The great Philadelphia 76er Allen Iverson once said, "I didn't take constructive criticism the way I should have. When I finally caught up to that, that's when I went to being the MVP." Like Iverson, they will begin to understand that criticism will be the difference between good and great. They will move from accepting criticism to actively seeking it out. This will be their secret ingredient, the piece that allows them to grow when others stagnate. It will be the lubricant that keeps them from getting stuck. As their comfort and mastery of the challenge advances, they will become skilled at who they seek criticism from, choosing mentors that embody the qualities they want to develop. They will not shy away from activities because of a fear of criticism, and this will lead to a broader and more well-rounded personality. They will move confidently in the presence of their superiors, knowing that any feedback they receive is intended to teach and not condemn.

Still Boarding

This student will be able to integrate criticism from people they like and in activities they like but will struggle outside of their comfort zone. They will most likely stick to activities that they already have a level of competence in, but even in these activities their growth will be minimal until they truly get comfortable with criticism from everyone, even the most brutally honest. They will struggle in areas they are less skilled in, maybe going as far as adopting the "I'm just not good at this" security blanket. They will be narrow in their skill set, developing above average skills in areas of interest and staying average to below average everywhere else. They will stay in this stunted state until they open themselves to criticism.

Flight Delayed

This student subscribes to the conspiracy theory that the world is out to get them. They perceive all criticism as a personal attack, and as a result will only do easy work. They will begin to fall behind those that are growing from feedback and may even resent them as a defense mechanism. They will likely develop a tendency to be defensive, constantly deflecting anything remotely resembling criticism, making them hard to work with. Relationships will be extra tricky as stronger emotions become intertwined with a situation that requires communication, feedback, and compromise. In the most severe cases, anything long-term will be next to impossible to maintain if their criticism deficiencies are not improved upon. Jobs, relationships, and even living arrangements will meet a boiling point when someone that cannot take criticism is asked to change, alter, improve, or discontinue a behavior.

PD for Parents & Teachers

For Parents

- How criticism is handled at home is going to be a factor in how your child receives criticism elsewhere. We must make sure our feedback to our children addresses behavior change (this is how to make your bed) and is not a personality attack (stop being such a slob).

- While your child is guaranteed to encounter teachers that are less than a standard you would hope for, try to help your child get as much as they can from every situation. Openly undermining the teacher's credibility through disparaging remarks may turn your child off to accepting anything the teacher has to offer. Help your child understand that while this teacher may not be at the top of their game, there is still something we can learn from everyone.

- Be a good model by being open to criticism from your family. This may require you asking for some (although, if you live with teenagers there will be plenty to respond to) but find ways to model listening and integrating criticism that comes your way. You may also be able to share examples from work on how your performance was improved by feedback from a co-worker or client.

For Teachers

- Embrace the warm demander persona. Be caring but strict. Have high expectations but offer support to get there. Be militantly organized and punctual and help your students to be the same. Our credibility as teachers (teacher credibility has a very high impact on student outcomes) is founded on how much we care about our students and how hard we work for them. Being a jerk (ridiculously high expectations, no care), a pushover (all love, no expectations), or a burnout (no expectations or care) diminishes outcomes.

- Grades are our students' scale, their data, so be good at producing them. Be efficient and fair in your systems, making sure that scores are going in regularly so that they can use that feedback to adjust their performance. Long lags can instill a false sense in students that they are doing ok. If a student checks their grades every morning and sees that they have a B+ in your class, but that B+ hasn't been updated in a month because you've let the work pile up, they believe whatever they've been doing this past month has kept them at a B+, even if that's not true. Imagine your bathroom scale is stuck at your preferred weight while you have been enjoying a donut every morning for breakfast. Wouldn't you rather have a scale that was working and letting you know what impact the daily donut was having on your weight? While your answer may be "no," the same goes for some of your students with a stuck grade, but that does not make it right or fair. Our scales should work.

- Be focused with your criticism. Students are going to produce work that has so many things wrong with it, but it is important to remember whatever the current objectives or areas of focus are, and to keep your feedback to those areas. We want them to improve, and to do that they have to be open and receptive to our feedback. If they get overwhelmed with too much, they will shut down. Essays are a great example of the need for focus and restraint in your feedback. Pick a couple areas of focus based on what you have been instructing and let everything else go for another time. What you let go may provide information on what needs to be the next topic of instruction.

Habits that Work for Teenagers

- **Every morning after I eat breakfast, I will check my grades online.** By stepping on the scale before school, students can make a list of teachers they need to see that day concerning anything that is missing, incorrectly scored, or upcoming that they may need assistance with.

- **Whenever the teacher/coach criticizes my performance, I will say "thank you" and begin doing it as they suggested.** By saying "thank you," students are acknowledging they have received the feedback positively. It also curtails the practice many have, which is to argue back. Instantly moving into the improved performance begins the process of solidifying the new act. If they are not able to perform the task immediately, they can visualize themselves doing it successfully as the teacher/coach suggested.

- **At the end of each week, I will ask my teacher/coach for one thing I can work on to improve.** The act of seeking out criticism regularly helps students see it as a normal, regular aspect of life. Criticism becomes as normal as breathing. And by regularly seeking and receiving feedback, students get in a rhythm of constant improvement, never stagnating.

Chapter Six

The Sixth Challenge: DEAL with DISCOMFORT

Good luck to you, even so. Farewell! But if you only knew, down deep, what pains are fated to fill your cup before you reach that shore.

From *The Odyssey* by Homer

Thomas Fuller, the English author, once said, "All things are difficult before they are easy." I handmade a poster with this quote some years ago when I came across it, and it is the only inspiration I have hanging on my classroom walls. If they can master this, the other nine challenges can fall like dominoes.

Pain and discomfort, and people's unwillingness to deal with them, may be the greatest barrier to anything in life. These are not the ten tasks, or the ten errands, and they are not even the ten tests. They are the ten *challenges* for a reason. Life is challenging, life is hard! If you are an adult reading this and you have achieved anything of value in life, you understand this completely. You also know that anything you have set out to achieve and have not, your unwillingness to deal with discomfort was likely why you were derailed. For most humans, success in life will be earned. Nothing is given.

The Sixth Challenge: DEAL with DISCOMFORT

High school is just practice for the game of life. I generally detest hokie sayings like, "Failure to prepare is preparing to fail," but that one hits the nail on the head. Oh jeez, I did it again.

High school is going to be full of challenging situations that require a student to endure some level of discomfort. It will present itself in many forms, and they all achieve the same end of placing students in unwelcome states. The arms that shake as they try to grunt out three more push-ups will combine with the potential embarrassment of not being able to do it, and a one-two punch of discomfort is landed. Getting better at anything requires repeated practice, which can lead to boredom, maybe the most insidious form of discomfort because it offers the plausible reason for stopping, "I'm bored." The pain of sacrifice has been amplified for today's teenagers because of social media and FOMO, the fear of missing out. Home is no longer the sanctuary of ignorance, where teens could unplug from the world outside and relax into their responsibilities. Now there's always evidence that some teen or group of teens are out there doing something ridiculous and way more fun than studying for an exam, all thanks to clueless parents that set no limits on their kids and make it extra difficult on those of us that do. The stress of pulling off the perfectly Instagramable promposal will detour many from ever experiencing prom altogether.

Mental challenges will make up the lion's share of the discomfort as students will be tasked with expanding their knowledge and academic skills. I'll address this in more detail in a later chapter, but how students deal with the challenge of expanding their "knowledge library," the store of accumulated information that they've taken the painful steps to remember, will significantly impact their level of access to the world as an adult. Since all new things are learned by connecting to things already learned, a small knowledge library can lead to much of the world being a confusing and scary place. These are the people that live in small bubbles, considering everything outside of them as "weird," "strange," and not to be trusted. These people say "no" a lot, mostly out of fear. Large knowledge libraries open the world as an exciting place of wonder and possibility. These people, that live in the big wide world that scares the small bubble people, are more inclined to say "yes" to life.

They will feel emotional and social discomfort as well. It is during this period where teenagers begin to separate from their parents and develop their identity, their personality, their character. They begin to experiment with style, and that will invite criticism. They will most likely fall for someone, and experience all the wild emotions associated with love[1]. They are most likely going to be rejected at some point if not several times, from individuals or groups of peers. They are going to be on teams and in groups with classmates they will need to work together with to accomplish a task or project. They will present their work in front of the class. All these situations are going to put your teen through the emotional and social wringer, and it is going to hurt. It will not always be painful, but it will be challenging, and it will require courage. And all of this is *just* the school stuff. Social media has rolled in like a fog and made navigating their academic life more challenging than for any generation prior. Unfortunately, I do not see the fog lifting any time soon.

The physical challenges will be there too. It would be nice if Physical Education were a four-year requirement, but it most likely is not where your child will attend. One or two years may be all that is required for graduation, with anything beyond that optional. It is here where the challenge manifests itself in its most basic form. Legs that feel dead, arms that begin to wobble, and chests that start burning are all sending a message to the brain, "please stop!" It is here, too, where students' responses to the challenge are most visible. As the class sets out on a mile run, everyone begins with a jog, but slowly, as the pain sets in, more and more begin to walk. The minutes continue to pass, and as more and more give in to their brain's request to end the discomfort, a pack of students at the front drive on, their faces grimacing. Their faces tell the story—this hurts, but I have a goal to achieve. The triumphant front runners cross the finish line and instantly double over or collapse onto the grass nearby in dramatic teenage fashion, and any pain they felt

---

[1] Admittedly, I come close to vomiting every time I hear a high school couple use the word "love" with their partner.

evaporates, replaced by a sense of joy, confidence, and accomplishment. They did it! And they know they can do it again.

And as they begin to sit up and take in the scene, they see those they left behind. The walkers, the ones that decided the discomfort was too much, will cross the finish line much later with excuses they have worked over in their head as to why their failure was justified. The excuses are necessary to soothe their ego, but they become dangerously easy to spin the more they get told.

Meanwhile, the runners are back on their feet, ready to run another mile if they were asked to. They have conquered the pain, and they have the confidence to conquer it again. And because they have, they will get faster and faster with each attempt.

Embrace, Then Change, The Climb

Sometimes a single word can make all the difference, and the most successful among us understand the power of words to shape attitudes, specifically their own. I remember reading about a school district that employed this philosophy by changing, "We need to feed our students," into, "We need to *nourish* our students." A single word led to an overhaul of how they operated their kitchens and the food they fed to their students. It went from the typical high starch and fat, blood sugar spiking, brain short circuiting foods normally found in school cafeterias, to locally sourced and healthy food that better prepared young bodies and minds for growth. Just one word changed the trajectory of all the students in that district.

In PE, most students can be heard complaining, "I *have* to run the mile today!" Meanwhile the best students silently step up to the line and prepare to work, their inner dialogue reminding them, "I *get* to run the mile today." A single word completely changing their whole disposition. They are not being forced; they are being *allowed* to exercise. This will not take forever; it will be over *quickly*. The teacher does not hate them, but instead *cares* about their well-being. Words matter, and often it only takes one.

Running the mile is the perfect metaphor for this challenge, and it is one I use often with my students because they all do it in high school. Next to algebra, it may be the most despised hoop of high school that everyone must jump through. When I use this metaphor to help students understand the nature of a challenge, I draw this on the board:

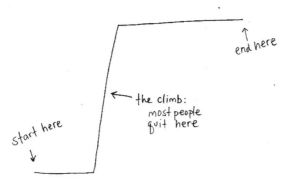

All challenges follow a similar pattern: easy at the start, followed by a period of discomfort (any combination of physical, mental, and/or emotional pain or struggle), followed by a breakthrough where the discomfort subsides and the finish line comes into view. It is here where runners experience their "runner's high," which I thought was a load of crap as a kid and just an excuse to encourage me to run. I don't possess a runner's frame (I'm almost 6'6" and 225 pounds), but I have committed to jogging as a form of exercise for some periods of my life, and when I was able to make it past the climb, I found out it was real. After feeling like I was going to lose control of all bodily functions and collapse into the gutter, a euphoria washed over me, and I felt like I could run forever.

Knowing the nature of a challenge, that after an easy start a period of discomfort will ensue, and preemptively assigning a positive word to it, will make all the difference in your ability to conquer the challenge. It was the great innovator Henry Ford that said, "Whether you believe you can, or you can't, you're right." He understood the power of words, and in his case, the power of a letter and an apostrophe.

When the changing of a word is challenging, noting how much worse it could be can help make the challenge seem not so bad. "I have to run the mile today," when compared to, "I have to work a twelve-hour shift in a third world sweatshop making shoes for twenty-five cents an hour," does not sound so bad. If given the choice of "doing thirty minutes of algebra homework," or "serving four years in a North Korean forced labor camp for a crime you didn't commit," algebra comes out on top.

Eventually, when successful people get to the point of embracing the climb they know is coming because the challenge is a necessary part of their growth and future, and they consistently make it to that euphoric plateau and finish line, they begin to change the climb. The more they face it, the more they climb it, the smaller it gets. Not only does it get smaller, but it happens later. Their progress looks something like this:

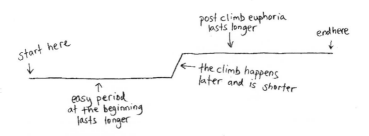

When they get to the flat line, they have mastered the challenge. Not only have they mastered the challenge, but they have mastered the process for successfully conquering all future challenges, just like Eddie did.

Eddie Would Go

I became aware of Eddie Aikau, the legendary Hawaiian lifeguard and surfer that perished while attempting to save the crew of a Polynesian sailing vessel, while I was living in Hawaii. A yearly big-wave surfing contest named in Eddie's honor is held only if the waves reach a minimum of twenty feet[2]. Early in its inception in the 1980s, contest organizers were contemplating cancelling the event because the conditions were too rough. Mark Foo, a big wave surfer that would later die while surfing the legendary big wave break Mavericks in California, told the organizers, "Eddie would go." Just like he had pulled so many to safety as a lifeguard on Oahu's famous North Shore, or how he attempted to save the crew of a sinking ship by paddling on his surfboard to land over twelve miles away, Eddie had a courage unmatched by many. The phrase, "Eddie would go," stuck, and bumper stickers and t-shirts can be seen all over Hawaii and the world, encouraging others to be brave, just like Eddie.

Years later I am in my first year of teaching high school, after ten years in middle school. I was teaching PE and English, and in a weight training class I had a student named Eddie. Eddie was the hardest working student I had ever seen in PE. Whenever we ran, no matter the distance or reason, he ran far and fast. The pain on his face as he pushed himself beyond anything expected of him was impressive. He lifted weights with intensity, unafraid to emit the sounds and make the expressions associated with extreme effort. I had never seen any student do anything as vigorously as Eddie worked out.

And then I looked at his grades.

To say Eddie was a poor student would do a disservice to the word "student." He had a D or F in every class except PE (where he had an A+, of course). This was his sophomore year, and he was already off track for graduation. He was going to need more than summer school to

---

[2] Which translates to a wave face of over thirty feet! Imagine a three to four story or larger building of thick, powerful ocean water barreling down on you, and you jump in!

get back on track, most likely transferring to an alternative high school designed for students like Eddie. Where I teach, transfers like this do not happen until after their sophomore year, and this was the midpoint of the Fall Semester. Eddie had three fourths of the year left before he was gone.

Eddie was not just a hard worker in PE. He had a great personality. He had a wide grin that was infectious, and he always got along great with his classmates. One day in PE class, shortly after learning of his grades, I pulled Eddie aside. I just wanted to let him know that I'd never seen anyone do anything with the intensity with which he exercised. I suggested that if he applied even a fraction of that effort to his academic courses, he would pass them. He knew how to work, he knew how to deal with discomfort, he just needed to apply it to more than PE. I did not expect what happened next.

Eddie listened.

Eddie's older brother had been to prison, and his parents worked in the fields of California's San Joaquin Valley, doing the back-breaking work of picking fruits and vegetables in temperatures routinely over one hundred degrees. They were Mexican immigrants that did not speak English. Prison or the fields were all Eddie ever imagined would be in his future. I encouraged him to give school a shot, to apply the same level of effort to writing essays as he did to push-ups. Ask for help with math, just like he did when he needed someone to spot him on the bench press or race him around the track. Just try it and see what happens.

He did just that.

Slowly the grades started to rise. He would excitedly share his progress, explaining how he had gone to tutoring and how he passed the test afterwards. He was learning how to use his talent for working, and it felt good. He was able to try out for the soccer team for the first time in his life because he was finally eligible academically. Although he had never played the sport beyond pick-up games in the park, he made an instant impact with his energy, earning the Coach's Award in his first year. In the semesters and years that followed, Eddie would go on to be an A and B student and a captain of the soccer team.

Eddie graduated high school, avoiding transfer to an alternative site by taking courses online to make up for failed classes earlier in high school. He moved onto the local junior college, where he continued to play soccer, and was again promoted to team captain. I would run into Eddie occasionally at the local gym, and he would catch me up on his progress. I always let him know how proud I was of him and how he earned it all through his effort. I had always let him know that I had still never encountered a student that worked as hard as he did. That would always make him smile his big, wide grin. Last time I saw Eddie he was successfully employed with a solar energy company and engaged to be married. No fields or prison for Eddie.

Like Eddie Aikau, the Eddie I encountered had courage that was inspiring. He had the courage to apply effort, an effort he had only applied to a field he enjoyed (exercise), to fields he had never had success in (every academic subject). He had the courage to ask for help. He had the courage to try. He had the courage to change his life.

I have told Eddie's story to just about every group of students I have had since. After telling them Eddie's story, I remind them how he would handle challenging situations that they had in front of them.

I simply let them know, "Eddie would go," and they can too.

Wrapping It Up

If you have ever been around children in their first year of life, you understand the importance of this challenge. I make it a point to ask students, "Did anyone come into this world walking and talking?" They will look at me quizzically, and I will rephrase, "Did anyone, on the day they were born, walk themselves out of the hospital and hop in the back seat of their parents' car?" We all have a good chuckle, before I get to my point. The answer is no, and most of my students have some experience being around babies and can help describe the determined effort infants put forth in their first year to move into toddlerhood. From crawling, to pulling themselves up to standing, to grasping the fingers of a hunched over family member, to those first drunken steps across the hopefully clutter free living room floor. Babies desperately want to walk, and there is no amount of discomfort they are unwilling to endure to make it so. Where would the teenagers sitting in front of me be if they had not dealt with the discomfort of learning how to walk? Or learn how to speak? Or any of the other skills they currently possess?

When those infants set out to become walkers, they had no idea where it would lead to. They could not imagine the running, jumping, and climbing skills that would develop upon mastery of walking. They just wanted to walk, but the effort put into its mastery opened a world of movement that further enhanced their enjoyment of life. For each skill we fail to develop through an unwillingness to deal with discomfort, how many more are we choking off before they get a chance to develop?

Dealing with discomfort in all its forms is an important challenge in a young person's development. Any worthwhile journey in life will be littered with obstacles, some like discarded cardboard that can be run over without slowing or changing course, and others like fallen logs across the road that require us to stop and recruit assistance to clear the path. If our teenagers are going to make it to their destination, they need the skills and courage to deal with these obstacles, and high school is where they can learn those skills and develop that courage.

Developing courage and strength is the cornerstone responsibility of a Hero's Journey, and it accomplishes this by testing individuals' capacity for dealing with discomfort. Conquering this challenge is a major indicator that a successful transition into adulthood is likely.

The Challenge's Impact on Trajectories

Ready for Take Off!

Students that exit high school having mastered this challenge broadly, in all aspects of their high school experience, have truly developed that quality popularized by Angela Duckworth's book of the same name, *Grit*. They have developed a passion for their long-term goals that have become increasingly real because of the success they achieved in high school. This passion fuels them through any inevitable discomfort they encounter on the way to their intended outcome. Sacrifice, a form of discomfort, becomes easy for them. They understand they can join their friends at the park playing basketball *after* they get done studying for tomorrow's algebra test, and they would not be able to enjoy playing otherwise. They have fully internalized the concept put forth by Carol Dweck in her groundbreaking book *Mindset*, that effort is the path to mastery. They know that of all the internal and external factors that will apply force on their trajectory, effort is the strongest of these forces and it is the one they control. This is powerful! Once they reach this point, everything truly becomes possible. Like the runners that finished first in high school, their work ethic and dedication will have them crossing the finish line as a member of the lead pack in any venture they get involved with after school. When things get difficult, when the pain starts asserting itself and the voices in their head start begging them to "stop!" they will not listen. They will block out the voices and call upon their reserves of effort they have built up over years of practice, and confidently finish the job again, and again, and again.

Still Boarding

Students that achieve partial success on this challenge will resemble those that had similarly mixed results with the previous challenge, embrace criticism. They were likely able to endure discomfort associated with activities that they enjoyed and from adults that they had positive relationships with but struggled elsewhere. Their developed skill set will reflect the balance of activities that they were willing to put the work into versus those they abandoned or fell short in. Even their strengths, already fewer than the Ready for Take Off! group, will not be as strong as they could be. To truly excel requires a level of practice and repetition that they were unlikely willing to commit to, maybe out of boredom. They were happy with being above average. This might lead to a regular pattern of abandoning projects or jobs in search of something novel, as the grind of a commitment becomes monotonous. In high school they may have also suffered from poor choice of pursuits, consistently choosing courses or activities that were too difficult or too easy, never finding that sweet spot just beyond their ability. In adulthood, they could see their trajectories take sudden and dramatic upward turns as they finally connect with projects and situations that match their ability and interests, keeping them properly challenged and engaged.

Flight Delayed

With these students, only the easiest and least challenging work will get done, and as a result their post high school prospects will be limited. Junior colleges will take them, but success here is unlikely unless some drastic behavior changes take place. All colleges, including junior and community colleges, require students to tackle difficult work, only now with greater independence and less support. Local Junior College is not going to call home when Johnny does not show up to school or has an F at the midpoint of the semester. Their great hope is that they find a field that somehow sparks their interest and gets them for the first time to continue working even when the influential (and to this point successful) voices in their head start begging them to put down the book and pick up the game controller. Barring this miracle, whatever jobs they get need to be easy, whatever relationships they have need to be easy, and whatever life demands of them, needs to be easy. People may eventually get annoyed when listening to them go on about their future, knowing that it is a pipe dream because work is involved. Their circle of friends will likely be other pasty, doughy, video game playing, hoodie and athletic attire wearing (because of the elastic waistbands and how they feel like pajamas, not because they actually exercise), parent's basement dwelling, pot smokers that will have their retired parents adding their name to birthday and Christmas gifts for an embarrassingly (to their parents, not them) long time. Maybe forever.

PD for Parents & Teachers

For Parents

- When your child accomplishes something, praise the effort they put into it and not the reward they earned. For example, instead of saying, "I'm so proud of your A in English," say, "I'm so proud of how hard you worked in English. You really grew this semester!"
- The world is full of inspiring stories of people overcoming incredible odds and dealing with great amounts of discomfort to achieve their goals, and many of these stories have been made into movies. Watch these types of movies with your family and make a point to highlight the grit and tenacity they showed in their pursuit.
- Model good word choice when talking about challenges you must deal with. You "get to work with" challenging customers that make life interesting. You "get to make a presentation" to the boss about areas where cuts need to be made. Our modeling goes a long way in shaping how our children process the world around them.

For Teachers

- If your students ever feel stuck, encourage them to just start working. Effort is the path to mastery, and effort is something they control. Just start working, and the solution will be found along the way. Be it writing or a set of math problems, they just need to get in motion, and once in motion they tend to stay there. If they are stuck because the amount of work seems overwhelming, help them pick one thing to complete first. A messy house can seem like too much to clean. Start by cleaning off the couch, and then clean off the table. The house gets cleaned one thing at a time.

- Praise work ethic, not intelligence. Focus your positive feedback on the effort students put into completing a task or solving a problem, and shy away from phrases like, "you're so smart."

- Get to know what your students are good at and help them see that they achieved their success by working hard and committing a lot of their time to it. This might be something like a sport, playing an instrument, drawing, or even playing video games. Help them to see that they got good at those activities by spending a lot of time doing them, and while these activities are ones they enjoy, the principle that anything is achievable through application of effort may start to take hold. It won't happen overnight (I wasn't the first teacher to give Eddie the "you can do better" speech), but the more they hear the message, the more it has a chance to take hold.

Habits that Work for Teenagers

- **On the ride to school each morning, I will think about the challenges I *get* to tackle that day.** By positively framing the challenges of the day as something they get to do instead of have to do, students proactively establish a positive mindset that is ready to run toward, instead of away from the day's difficult work.

- **When it is time to register for classes, I will choose courses that are not too easy or too difficult.** Known as the Goldilocks Rule, we are at our peak engagement when the challenge is "just right," not too easy to bore us, or not too difficult to exasperate us. Hitting the sweet spot in course selection is an undervalued skill.

- **Before I begin work on a challenging task, I will remind myself of challenging tasks I have accomplished in the**

past. A little boost of confidence and motivation is like a triple shot of espresso in the afternoon. Reminding ourselves of how far we have come by looking back, makes looking forward and soldiering on more doable. Sometimes the best source of self-inspiration to work hard *today*, comes from the realization that it will take us to heights we would otherwise miss out on in the *future.*

Chapter Seven

The Seventh Challenge: LEARN

The more that you read, the more things you will know, the more that you learn, the more places you'll go.

From *I Can Read with My Eyes Shut!* by Dr. Seuss

Our brains are what set us apart as the dominant species on the planet. If it was a world built on physical strength, then elephants, gorillas, or tigers would rule. Whales, orca, and sharks would rule the oceans (as they do now, I guess). We would be specimens in their zoos. At least for the time being, until we get fooled into outsourcing all our knowledge to Google and the robots take over, we are in charge. And while we are in charge, we need to do everything in our power to develop our brains to stay there.

As I mentioned previously, all learning is dependent on prior learning. What you have already learned will be the foundation for what you can learn. Imagine a game of Jenga, where rectangular wooden blocks are stacked to make a tower with three blocks laid side by side to make a single "story," and instead of removing a block from a lower level and moving it to the top as the game is normally played, you merely placed a fresh block to the top. The solid foundation would remain intact, and you just had to build upward. The game would be easy and could go on indefinitely because a solid foundation remained intact. This is how successful students' brains grow, by placing new knowledge on a solid foundation of previously learned knowledge.

Now imagine Jenga as it is normally played, where blocks from below are removed and placed on the top, creating a precariously teetering tower as the game continues. Eventually there comes a point where a block is removed and placed on top, and somewhere in that process the whole tower comes tumbling down. Poor students continually live in this mental state, where the tower is going to collapse at any moment because they are trying to balance something new on top of something fragile. Their towers collapse so often, they stop even trying to build up.

One of the stronger arguments for the value of education comes from the data connecting rates of unemployment to the level of education attained. Reports consistently show that the more educated you are, the less likely you are to experience unemployment. While I started writing this during a period of low unemployment and stable economic growth, the coronavirus pandemic has caused an unprecedented surge in unemployment claims. Many businesses may never reopen as a result of the tumult caused by our effort to thwart the virus' spread, and all their employees will be forced to look for new employment in very long lines of job seekers. It is hard to believe that just over a decade prior to our current calamity, unemployment rates doubled during the Great Recession of 2007 to 2009. In both instances, the level of education an individual has earned has factored heavily into whether they have been able to weather the storm. But why is that?

Imagine a continuum of education from top to bottom, the top being the most educated and the bottom the least educated, that looks like this:

Professional Degree*
Doctoral Degree
Master's Degree
Bachelor's Degree
Associates Degree

Certificate Program**
High School Diploma
Graduate Equivalency Diploma (GED)
Less than GED

* Professional Degrees refer to the education required to go into fields like medicine and law.
** Certificate Programs usually take less than two years, sometimes less than one, and focus on a single skill like welding or cosmetology

People tend to want to work at the highest level their education will allow. Not only is the pay usually better[1], but the jobs that match your level of education are more likely to provide the kind of challenge that keeps you engaged. It is unlikely that someone that earned a Doctorate is going to apply for a job as a grocery bagger, and a high school graduate has no place applying for a management position. Not only would the Doctor be intellectually bored out of their mind by the daily tasks of a grocery bagger, but his hourly wage would not make a dent in the school loans he or she racked up earning the Doctorate.

But, could the Doctorate earner apply for the grocery bagger position? Yes, they could, and during the Great Recession there were many instances of highly educated people taking jobs well below their level of ability. In times of crisis, you do what you must do to keep money coming in.

Who got hurt the worst? The lower educated individuals that were being bumped out of positions by those above them. The phenomena we're experiencing now as a result of the coronavirus pandemic, is that businesses that are being forced to shutter, like restaurants and retail stores, are largely staffed by lower wage workers that tend to have lower levels of education.

Education, and the knowledge gained while becoming educated, opens the world up. For years, being a fry cook at McDonald's somehow became the worst job in the world as evidenced by how many times it

---

[1] Another argument for the value of education.

was used as a threat for those in danger of not doing well in school. "You're going to end up making fries at McDonald's for the rest of your life!" could be heard in classrooms across America by teachers frustrated with students that were not doing their work. McDonald's fry cook became the symbol of the type of entry-level, no prior skills required, minimum wage jobs many teenagers would earn as their first job. The threat was an implication that they would never progress from there.

I always found this threat to be insensitive, and you do not hear it so much anymore as we have evolved as a society and are more aware of how our words and actions may be offensive and wrong. The truth is, for some, being a McDonald's fry cook is the best job in the world. They experience a real sense of flow, they enjoy serving customers, they work with a great crew, they love their boss, they're proud to be a part of such an iconic American brand, they love the fast-paced energy that makes the day move along, and it meets their financial needs. The only person that is truly threatened by a lifetime spent hunched over boiling grease is the one that dreamt of something greater, failed to develop themselves, and is stuck in the only job they qualified for and they have to work at to pay the bills (which are most likely shared with others). They are miserable everyday as they put on their uniform and head off to work.

Imagine you have been driving for miles without any signs of civilization. It has been almost twenty-four hours since your last meal and you are famished. You see a diner in the middle of nowhere and you begin to salivate as you pull into the parking lot. You run inside, throw yourself into a booth and grab the menu that has been left on the table. To your surprise, there is one food item on the menu, meatloaf. It comes with a side of mashed potatoes and peas. No substitutions. Root beer and coffee are the only beverage choices besides water. The menu lists just one dessert item. But when the waitress meanders over, her first words are, "We're fresh out of our cherry pie. Sorry."

If you are a fan of meatloaf and root beer, you might think you just crossed over into heaven. What are the chances! Most people, however, while thankful to finally get some food in their belly, will be extremely disappointed by the lack of choices. Vegetarians are majorly bummed.

Not learning things and getting an education is kind of like that, a roll of the dice. You are going to have fewer choices, and you might get lucky and find something you will love doing for the rest of your life. Or you could be the vegetarian forced to consider meatloaf.

Education gives you a full menu, and the more you earn, the longer the menu of choices grows. It also means you can change your mind later if you get tired of eating the same thing all the time.

High school is going to expose students to so much information, so many facts, so many ways to solve problems, so many questions to ponder. The more a student approaches high school like preparation for *Jeopardy!* where brainiacs miraculously regurgitate facts about an extremely broad range of topics, the better off they will be. There is no downside to learning new things, and only tremendous upside.

Committing newly learned information to memory, and then being able to recall that newly learned information in the service of solving problems or understanding something completely new, is the door to an educated life. Mastering how to memorize and recall information is the key that opens that door.

NOTE: The sections that follow, "You Can't Just Google It'" and "The Five Best Ways to Learn New Material" are admittedly technical and may seem a little detached from the rest of the book. While I considered altering or removing them entirely to achieve greater cohesion, their value is just too important to omit. Understanding how the brain works, and more importantly how it grows, is knowledge all mentors should possess. It is our job, as parents and teachers, to design activities that help those in our charge grow to their potential. If we fail to take the time to understand how the brain operates, then we will be less effective in our primary duty, and our teens will be the ones that suffer. Please take these next two sections to heart, become an expert on how brains learn and grow, and refine how you craft projects intended to help your junior heroes develop into the best possible versions of themselves. Any of the books mentioned in these sections would be worthwhile reads for those wishing to dive deeper into the science behind the subject.

You Cannot "Just Google It"

The "just Google it" argument assumes that our brains function like computers. It posits that the "old school" notion of remembering vast stores of information is a relic of a bygone era (my grandfather could recite poems he memorized in grade school until the day he passed). It argues that like computers, we do not really need to commit to memory anything that we believe will not need to be recalled and used repeatedly. All we need to learn are processes of thinking, and when we need to feed some information through these processes, we will "just Google it." Peddlers of this argument believe this is the Information Age, with information readily available at the click of a button, so why waste time remembering any of it? Outsource it to the cloud![2]

The swinging pendulum has rendered ideas like "rote memorization" and "drill and kill" taboo in current educational thinking, and it is having the adverse effect that often comes with extreme responses: students are not memorizing *anything*. No need to memorize anything kids, we have a class set of Chromebooks!

While I am less fearful of this happening at the elementary level because teachers there understand deeply the need for stored, factual knowledge, there is growing evidence the "just Google it" mentality is spreading at higher levels of education. Unfortunately, this philosophy is being pushed by adults that grew up remembering things and seem to discount the value of their memories as they have entered the Information Age. There are four reasons why this is problematic.

---

[2] Over dinner with a friend that is a parent of teenagers and a lawyer, this topic came up and it struck a nerve. He had become frustrated with the recent hires and had started referring to the new crop of lawyers at his firm as "Google Lawyers," because they didn't seem to have any important case history memorized, instead relying on Google to look everything up. As a result, they were less effective and creative in their argumentation. Their brains lacked experience *and* stored knowledge, and as a result their thinking was labored and flat.

First off, prior knowledge is required to learn something new. Joshua Foer writes in *Moonwalking with Einstein* that, "Even if facts don't by themselves lead to understanding, you can't have understanding without facts. And crucially, the more you know, the easier it is to know more." In *Make it Stick* by Peter C. Brown, Henry L. Roediger III, and Mark A. McDaniel, they add that, "All new learning requires a foundation of prior knowledge."

When I started teaching over twenty years ago, "activating prior knowledge" was such a commonplace phrase, you were hard pressed to read a pedagogical article that did not include it. It has been replaced with "just Google it."

This shift is highly problematic because anyone that has spent time teaching young people how to read knows the importance of prior knowledge to the process. The brain cannot understand new information if it does not have something already stored in the brain to relate it to. Literal connections grow in the brain when new information is processed and connected to existent information, creating a more complex weave of stored knowledge.

"The more you know, the more you can know" is also a forgotten adage when this new argument is pushed. Do not mistake information with knowledge. If two students Google the same topic, and one of them has much more stored information in their head, will they be able to understand, process, and use the Googled information equally? Not on your life.

Secondly, working memory functions better with larger, memorized "chunks." In one of my favorite books about learning, *Why Don't Students Like School*, Daniel T. Willingham states, "The phenomenon of tying together separate pieces of information from the environment is called chunking. The advantage is obvious: you can keep more stuff in working memory if it can be chunked. The trick, however, is that chunking works only when you have applicable factual knowledge in long-term memory...Thus, background knowledge allows chunking, which makes more room in working memory, which makes it easier to relate ideas, and therefore to comprehend." Barbara Oakley backs this up in *A Mind for*

Numbers with, "The bigger your chunked mental library, the more easily you will be able to solve problems."

Working memory, which is where thinking takes place, can only hold about four pieces of information at a time. When a child is first learning to read, those pieces are individual letters and the sounds they make, like "c," "a," and "t." Just those three letters push their working memory to its capacity. Eventually this becomes the chunk "cat," freeing up working memory space for other words and greater understanding of text. These chunks live in our brain because we took the time to understand them. Again, from *Moonwalking With Einstein* by Joshua Foer, "...when it comes to chunking—and to our memory more broadly—what we already know determines what we're able to learn."

When we take the time to remember new things and connect it to prior learning, we are creating larger and more complex chunks of information. In the future, when we are asked to apply higher order thinking to a new topic, the more complex the chunks are that we pull into working memory from long term memory, the better our thinking will be. Whatever you Google will be new and pulling it into working memory will require you do so in small chunks. Those small chunks will max out your working memory quickly.

Next, deep understanding and higher order thinking require memory. In *Why Don't Students Like School*, Willingham adds that, "The processes we most hope to engender in our students—thinking critically and logically—are not possible without background knowledge." In *Make it Stick*, Brown, Roediger III, and McDaniel contribute, "...for without knowledge you don't have the foundation for the higher-level skills of analysis, synthesis, and creative problem solving...Mastery requires both the possession of ready knowledge and the conceptual understanding of how to use it."

The greater our store of knowledge, the more deeply we will understand new information. As new information enters the brain, it is first processed in working memory with its limited capacity. This is where we think about it and connect it with what we already know. The larger our chunks are and the more connections we can make to prior learning, the deeper and better we understand this new information. This deeper understanding leads to better analysis and manipulation of the information, and more creative and effective outcomes. Put simply, you cannot think deeply about something you just Googled.

Lastly, memory is what makes us human. In *Moonwalking With Einstein*, Foer concludes that, "...who we are and what we do is fundamentally a function of what we remember." In *Brain Rules* by John Medina we get, "Most researchers agree that its (memory's) influence on our brains is what truly makes us consciously aware."

Our memories make us who we are. The information we hold in our head helps us to process the world, make decisions, and learn lessons from our mistakes. Our personality is intimately connected with what we know, informing the words we select in our conversations and our reactions in the moment.

Let me leave you with this one last warning from *The Shallows: What the Internet is Doing to Our Brains* by Nicholas Carr:

"Of all the sacrifices we make when we devote ourselves to the Internet as our universal medium, the greatest is likely to be the wealth of connections within our own minds."

The Five Most Effective Ways to Learn New Material

Learning requires practice, but not all practice produces learning. At the most basic level, teachers are tasked with helping their students learn new things, so it is reasonable to assert that teachers should be experts at practice. It also stands to reason that parents, the most important teachers a child will ever have, should be well-versed in the types of practice that most effectively produce growth. While it may be reasonable to assert such claims, the truth may not square with reason.

The past few decades have seen quantum leaps in our understanding of how the brain operates, especially how it learns, retains, and uses new information. Researchers and scientists the world over have conducted countless projects and experiments that have yielded a strong database from which to make informed, concrete suggestions about the ways that we, and more importantly our students and children, learn new material. This very brief synopsis culls together the five most effective ways to organize practice for learners. These five types of practice—retrieval, spaced, interleaved, elaboration, and generation—have undergone rigorous testing, and these tests have been replicated many times. Not only do they work, but they are free and require no technology. While technology may be used to enhance or augment some of these strategies, it is not required. Anyone can do them anywhere.

1. Retrieval

This strategy uses regular tests and quizzes to force the recall of learned material, and it works best when it is low stakes and the intent is learning.

Retrieval works by forcing the brain to recall information from long-term memory, and then strengthening connections to prior knowledge when the information gets reconsolidated. Also, the learner becomes aware of areas of weakness that need attention. The more this happens the better. Think of a football team that plays 10 games in a season, 1 per week, with practices during the week between games. Now imagine a team that practices for 10 weeks and then plays 1 game. Which team is going to be better prepared for the play-offs that start in week 11? The second team never gets a chance to use the games (tests) to improve, to challenge their recall, or to find out their weaknesses and shore them up. While this situation (practicing 10 weeks to play 1 game) seems preposterous for those that understand sports (and probably even those that don't), how many of our classrooms are set up this way?

2. Spaced

This strategy uses the distribution of learning over time as opposed to cramming. The same amount of material is covered and the same amount of time is spent, but it is chopped up into shorter periods spread out with time in between (for example, 20 minutes of studying spread out over 3 days, versus 1 hour of studying on 1 day).

Spaced learning works because it builds in desirable difficulty by allowing some "forgetting" to take place. When the material is pulled out of long-term memory and reconsolidated, connections are strengthened and multiplied, because new connections are made with material learned since the previous session. This repeated recall and reconsolidation process embeds the knowledge in a way that makes it more retrievable for a longer period, becoming a more solid foundation for future learning. The learner also benefits from the sleep in between sessions to help consolidate and make sense of the new material. Cramming on the other hand, while effective for an immediate test, is ineffective for long-term knowledge building. If a big test were to be delayed, the crammer would be in trouble while the spacer would not.

3. Interleaved

This strategy utilizes the practice of mixing the types of problems to be solved instead of focusing on a single type of problem and doing a lot of them (massed practice).

This technique works because in the opposite situation, when a single type of problem is done repeatedly, the problem solver's need to discriminate the type of skill and/or knowledge required to solve the problem is stripped of them. This makes it easier for the learner, but easier is not better. Difficulty is desired for better learning and having to think about how to solve a problem before attempting to solve it strengthens the learning process. Also, real-life and comprehensive exams are not like massed practice. While learners experience greater success during a massed practice session, they do significantly worse on comprehensive exams when there is a need to discriminate what type of skills and knowledge are needed to solve disparate problems. One study had some baseball players participate in massed batting practice by hitting 15 fastballs, 15 curveballs, and 15 changeups in that order (this was their, and most teams, normal way of practicing). Another group hit the same amount of balls (45), and the same number of each type (fastball, curveballs, and changeups), but in an interleaved, random fashion. While the massed practice hitters fared better in practice, the interleaved hitters did significantly better in games when the need to discriminate what type of pitch is being thrown is vital for success. The massed practice hitters had not developed that ability because in practice they knew what type of pitch was coming.

4. Elaboration

In this strategy, learners are encouraged to express and explain, as deeply as possible, their understanding of newly acquired knowledge or skills in their own words. The learner may respond to a specific question posed by the instructor or may participate in general reflection. (Note: this is not summarization)

It works because the process of reflecting and elaborating on newly learned material forces the learner to discover salient points and key concepts, and to make connections with previously learned material. This increases the number of connections and cues the learner must later recall the newly learned material. This process also becomes richer as the learner creates personal metaphors for the new material, and/or creates mental images that increase the strength and later recall of the learning.

5. Generation

In this final strategy, learners are presented with a problem prior to having learned the skills necessary to solve it. Learners are asked to apply whatever knowledge or skills they may have that they believe can help them solve it.

It works because without the exact skills or knowledge necessary to solve a problem, learners activate prior, related knowledge and begin searching for connections. This search, and the subsequent application of whatever they come up with, primes the pathways in the brain that will eventually be home to the new learning necessary to solve the new problem. When the learner is presented with the necessary skills or knowledge, the learning is stronger and more durable when applied to the previously unsolvable problem (creating a lightbulb, "aha" moment). This process also utilizes the concept of "desirable difficulty," inducing a struggle in the learner that aids in consolidation of new material.

You may have noticed that arguably the most used form of practice, massed, where learners repeat the same skill over and over until it becomes fluent did not make the top five. The fact is it would not even be considered number six.

Massed practice has a place, but it is limited and does not deserve the prestigious post it currently holds. While massed practice feels good, because fluency with a skill increases quickly, this fluency does not translate into real-world contexts where multiple strategies are necessary. Massed and blocked[3] practices have a place when a learner is first becoming familiar with a skill, but this type of practice should soon be replaced with one of the five types mentioned above, especially one of the first three. Our addiction to massed practice is well-entrenched, and most people mistakenly believe that they learn best in this fashion. Even the baseball players that practiced in an interleaving fashion and later outperformed their massed practice teammates, later believed that they learned best in a massed pattern, despite firsthand proof otherwise!

The simple fact is that many research studies have been conducted, and they all come to the same conclusion: massed practice, while it feels good and produces minor long-term gains, should take a backseat to these other, way more effective types of practice. Learning is better when there is a desirable amount of difficulty, and massed practice too quickly removes the challenge of having to discern which strategy or steps to apply. As a result, the learner skips this vital step and goes on cruise control, solving the same problem type over and over. Also, because the brain is accessing information repeatedly from short-term, working memory, instead of retrieving and reconsolidating information from

---

[3] Where learners do problem sets in blocks—think of the batters doing 45 hits, 15 at a time against each type of pitch.

long-term memory (which happens during retrieval, spaced, and interleaved practice), the new skills are not embedded as deeply and effectively as they are in other types of practice.

Wrapping It Up

We all know that guy or girl that seems to know everything. You may work with them, be friends with them, be related to them, or maybe even married to them. In fact, it might be you. There doesn't seem to be a conversation topic they can't contribute to, a problem they don't have a reasonably effective solution for (and one they arrive at much quicker than anyone else), or activity they can't jump into and not appear moronic. They are comfortable with any group in any arena, and they easily and excitedly move from setting to setting with an almost giddy sense of curiosity and joy. New environments and people are not scary to them, and in fact they are the exact opposite. They know, because of the vast knowledge library they have developed over their lives, that they have the capacity to learn and adapt quickly to anything new, and this makes the world an exciting place full of potential and opportunity.

I do not know about you, but this is what I dream for my two children, and all the young people I teach.

In *The Teenage Brain: A Neuroscientist's Survival Guide to Raising Adolescents and Young Adults* written by Frances E. Jensen, MD with Amy Ellis Nutt, they point out that "even the average human brain is said by many scientists to be the most complex object in the universe." They go on to emphasize the importance of taking brain development seriously during high school by sharing that "there is solid data to show that your IQ can change during your teen years, more than anyone had ever expected. Between thirteen and seventeen years of age, one-third of people stay the same, one-third of people decrease their IQ, and a remarkable one-third of people actually significantly raise their IQ...teens need to become aware this is one of the golden ages for their brains!" Leave it to an ivy league neuroscientist to get exclamative about teenage brain development, but the evidence is clear, and the consequences are immense, so can you blame her?

Our brains are magnificent organs that during the teenage years, are begging to be stuffed full of information and experiences, tasked with solving the unsolvable, and challenged with creating the new and wonderful world that exists in their imagination. It is truly a "golden age" of growth, but only if the challenge to learn is accepted and approached with vigor. Consider yourself lucky if the heroes you are tasked with mentoring step up to this challenge willfully. For most of us, we will need to dig deep into our motivational tool kit, and we will need to prepare ample reserves of patience. While it may be *a* golden age for brain development, it is *the* golden age of raging hormones and irrational choices.

The world, and everyone's opportunity to live their richest life possible within it, will expand or contract depending on the energy put into learning.

The Challenge's Impact on Trajectories

Ready for Take Off!

This student, in simplest terms, is smart. As described previously, their broad base of knowledge will allow them to fearlessly enter new arenas and situations knowing that there is something in their knowledge library that will help them make sense of this place and adapt quickly. They will also rise at an above average clip because their store of information increases their processing speed, and because they have mastered advanced methods for absorbing and using new facts and skills. Their ability to craft solutions to problems will make them an asset in any group, particularly in work settings where their ability to suggest more effective systems or more creative marketing campaigns will make them invaluable. All these potential trajectories, however, demand that this challenge not be conquered in isolation, which it sometimes does. The brilliant underachiever is one of the most frustrating students any teacher ever comes across because of their immense potential. They possess a predilection for learning and an abhorrence for work. They will sit in front of the TV and rattle off answer after answer while watching *Jeopardy!* (while probably wearing athletic attire and eating directly from a large bag of chips), but could never put it together to go through the steps to apply for and audition for the show (quite possibly because it would require wearing clothes with zippers and buttons). It is imperative that this challenge not be mastered in isolation, but instead combined with others, namely the previous one, *Deal with Discomfort*, and the next one, *Produce*. Brains and work ethic are an insanely lethal combination. Brains alone, not so much.

Still Boarding

This may be the one challenge where many people that land here end up overseeing people that finish in the Ready for Take Off! group. IQ, the measure of a person's intelligence, while not fixed, does have its limits for growth. If LeBron James were 5'8", he would be a very different LeBron James. Part of what makes him the most dominant force in basketball on the planet for his generation, is that he is not 5'8", but instead 6'8". He took the gift of his size and combined it with an insane work ethic to become who he is. The work ethic is the key, and I have no doubt the 5'8" LeBron, had he worked as hard as the 6'8" LeBron, would still be successful, just maybe not at basketball. Not every 6'8" kid becomes LeBron. So, what does this mean for your kid? As a teacher, I absolutely LOVE my hard working students that I can tell struggle a little more with learning new things (because they were born with a 5'8" brain), and get absolutely frustrated with students that learn new stuff easily (because they were born with a 6'8" brain), but won't do a lick of work. Students in this category are likely not straight A students, but if every grade was truly a reflection of their best effort (and occasionally that is going to be a C), then they are going to survive. They may experience some limits, but if they have developed good work habits, they will overcome them.

Flight Delayed

I almost do not even want to write this section. The thought of exiting high school with an incredibly small knowledge library fills me with great sorrow. I cannot imagine a life where so much of it is confusing and scary. There also exists one of my least favorite types of people in this group, the overly-confident-but-doesn't-know-much guy. This is the person that was pumped with shockingly large doses of praise from their family, but never held accountable for any level of performance. They were the prince or princess that floated through high school and life on a cloud of excuses and temper tantrums. Their arguments make you want to scream to the high heavens they are so devoid of reason and facts, yet they are peddled and defended so vigorously and without shame. There also exists the shut in, the one afraid to do anything because the world is so foreign and strange. Nothing makes sense, and this leads to a paralysis that is impossible to shake. See why I did not want to write this section?

PD for Parents & Teachers

For Parents

- Modeling the behaviors we want our children to develop is our most powerful tool of influence. We must be curious and courageous in the face of all things new, and we should seek it out. Around the dinner table and on weekend outings, what we say and the activities we plan will make a world of difference.
- Encourage non-tech study methods, like good old-fashioned flash cards for retrieval practice. Your child's devices will have 21st Century versions of flash cards that they will want to use

on their phone or laptop, but this is also the place (their device) where they watch videos and check social media. They will be more focused, and more effective without the distractions.

- Make sure that your child is enrolled in activities that offer the proper amount of challenge, increasing the likelihood they develop a work ethic to go along with their intelligence. If courses are too easy, and they can pass with good enough grades with little or no effort, they are going to be in for a world of hurt post high school. Developing their work habits alongside their intelligence is the combination that will prevent stalls in their trajectory.

For Teachers

- Curate facts and terms that students must commit to memory. For each chapter or unit, have a vocabulary list and other facts that are essential for them to add to their knowledge library. Do not forget that Webb's Depth of Knowledge (DOK) and Bloom's Taxonomy are built on a foundation of remembering and building knowledge. You cannot synthesize or analyze what you do not know.

- Use daily, low stakes quizzing. A great way to do this would be to start a Google Slides called "Daily Quiz," and each slide has five questions on it. The questions are a mix of everything learned to this point, with three questions focused on material recently learned, and two coming from material further back. By consistently having to forage through their knowledge library to find information, students will get better at knowing where stuff is and finding it quicker.

- Teach them how to study for tests. If you find students are not studying, make it an assignment. Create study guides that can be folded in half (questions on the left, answers on the right) and used like flash cards. Commit time in class to studying and make studying and committing information to memory a big deal, because it is.

Habits that Work for Teenagers

- **Whenever I have new information I need to memorize, I will make flashcards and quiz myself.** The deliberate act of quizzing yourself, forcing your brain to recall new information again and again is the most effective way to learn anything. By committing to it, habitually, the process will become more effective as the new information has more and more to connect to.

- **Every night before I go to bed, I will spend two minutes journaling everything new I learned that day.** A consistent habit, that only takes two minutes, of reflecting and jotting down whatever was learned in a day prepares the brain for an incredibly effective night of organization. Like a dream journal—the practice of immediately journaling whatever dreams you had immediately after waking to develop your ability to more regularly and clearly remember them—a learning journal aids in the retention of newly learned material.

- **Whenever I encounter something new, I will make a mental list of the ways it is like things I already know.** The act of relating the unknown to the known is not only how the act of learning works, but it alters how new things are perceived. It takes something that may be scary and turns it into the familiar. This mindset keeps those that adopt it from becoming trapped in small bubbles.

Chapter Eight

The Eighth Challenge:
PRODUCE

All we have to decide is what to do with the time that is given us.

From *The Fellowship of the Ring* by J.R.R. Tolkien

Parents and teachers of teenagers are constantly challenging them with how to spend their time, just like Gandolf did to Frodo before he and his band set out on their quest. And as Gandolf conceded in the quote that begins this chapter, nobody can be forced to undertake a quest; *they* must decide to do it if the results are to be true.

Mastery of this challenge may be the surest way any teenager has of warding off a failed launch into adulthood. If they can develop that worker mindset, the one that has them respond to requests for work in an almost Pavlovian manner, the request triggering every cell of their being to commit immediately to the task at hand before returning to their previous duties, they will always find a spot on the team. It is the worker mindset that provides the forward thrust of our trajectories, like jet engines on a plane, while the other nine challenges act like the wings, tail, and flaps that manipulate that thrust. Without the engines, however, you have a beautifully crafted feat of engineering that just sits there and looks good, unable to fulfill its ultimate purpose. Without the engines, a plane is just its potential.

While this is one of the more straightforward challenges, which in its simplest form is "do work," it is also one where we see the greatest resistance because, well, they are teenagers. At a time in their lives when greater independence and mobility are emerging, and in an era where technology allows them to stay continuously tethered to their peers, asking teenagers to abandon everything they desire to be doing and commit to the last thing they want to do—like compose an essay or complete a set of algebra problems—is a huge ask. But this is part of the challenge! Like Frodo on his quest to safely deposit the ring in the fires of Mount Doom to save Middle Earth, the journey is intentionally harrowing and difficult. Frodo, an unassuming Hobbit just chilling in the beautiful Shire is suddenly the Ring Bearer? It is how heroes are made! Where would our planet be if high school tasks included things like sleep in until noon, eat a donut or two, put your headset on and play a few hours of video games, and then use the rest of the day to either watch YouTube or Netflix? Yeah, that's how important high school is. It stands between the future that moves our species forward and the future imagined in *WALL-E*, the great Pixar flick that depicts an earth uninhabitable because of the accumulated trash, where obese humans spend their days on hovering chaise loungers, their faces glued to screens as they suck on Big Gulps, all while the robots plan their takeover. Sounds funny, and it was, but it also seemed frighteningly possible.

While "do work" is the challenge simplified, there are some qualifying words that help make the challenge a little clearer. "Do work now" implies the importance of immediacy, and how the best workers are not procrastinators. "Do good work" shines a light on the need for work to be done with quality in mind if the worker is going to be recognized for their craft. "Do extensive work" indicates that the size or amount of our product will matter at times, and the need to put greater effort and time into creating work of length will be important. "Do work together" is going to be an invaluable facet of the challenge to master, one that will bring many of the best workers to their knees when paired with work-averse teammates. "Do pointless/boring/disconnected work" illuminates an unfortunate reality of life, that we sometimes need to put our head down and do the work in front of us, even when it lacks perceived value.

Students are going to be asked to do *a lot* of work in high school, more than they have ever been asked to do before. They are also likely to be involved in more extra-curricular activities than ever before, which will load even more work and more demands on their time. They are also going to experience more independence, when they and/or their friends begin to drive or use public transportation autonomously, fueling a desire to go out and explore the world free from their parents. All these things will come together, pushing and pulling them in every direction, forcing them to make decisions about how they allocate their time and their energy. Kind of sounds like life as we know it, doesn't it?

High school is their training ground for life, and amidst all the temptations, distractions, and expectations, they are going to need to prioritize work. We all know the value of this, and we have found ways to manage our time and balance our responsibilities to get whatever work we do that pays the bills done. It is an important part of life. Makes sense that it is an important part of high school.

Getting Things Done

There is probably no better resource for how to be a workflow master than David Allen's *Getting Things Done*. It has a cult-like following for good reason; the principles and systems contained within its pages are utilized by some of the most productive and successful people in the world, that tackle mountains of work that would crush mere mortals, and do so stress free. It is not just some general principles about how to be organized, but a complex and exact system that requires some practice and investment to get up and running. Once internalized, you will be amazed at the output you are capable of.

The Eighth Challenge: PRODUCE

I will admit that I am not a strict follower of the GTD program. My life just does not demand that I employ elaborate systems to stay on top of the work required of me. I do, however, regularly utilize a couple of the principles and systems that I believe anyone would benefit from, regardless of the workload.

The principle that I learned from Mr. Allen that has had the most profound impact on not just my ability to more efficiently handle work, but to think better, is the act of decluttering your mind by writing down and collecting all of those ideas, appointments, and tasks swirling around in your head. For example, I have been collecting all the ideas for this book for years completely in my head. I did not know it at the time, I was merely observing, thinking, reading, and talking about all these topics until they became an overwhelming mass I had to deal with. Then I remembered this concept from GTD, went to the store to gather some pens, notepads, and an accordion folder with tabs, and upon returning home started dumping everything out of my head and onto notepad paper that I could rip off once I had filled a page. I did this for days as thoughts and ideas that were wedged into the corners came loose and floated to the surface. By the end of it, I had several books worth of ideas, the first of which you are reading now. I sat down and organized the ideas into books and then into chapters, and then I filed those papers into the accordion file to be accessed when I need them. With my mind now free of that huge mass of ideas, the efficiency of my writing is effortless. I've composed the equivalent of a 150 page essay in just over a month in my spare time, an hour here and an hour there, but I couldn't have done it if I hadn't collected the ideas on paper and cleared my head.

Students need to write things down. Due dates, essay ideas, upcoming exams, or whatever school and life related thoughts and information they come across or conjure in their heads. They should have a system, preferably one that includes a notebook for collecting notes and ideas, and a calendar or planner for keeping important dates. I am going to put my grandpa slippers on here and suggest these collection tools be non-tech. I know our devices have incredible workflow solutions, but the more we can separate where we play and where we work, the better. By habitually taking out their notepad or planner whenever information enters their brain, and then sorting that information into a place where they know it is safe and accessible, the freer their minds will be to think, create, and produce. It is like keeping a house clean, and how good it makes you feel. If you have systems in place to keep it from ever becoming a mess in the first place[1], you don't end up like one of those frozen wrecks on the horrific reality show *Hoarders* (which my wife Laurie loves and I can't bear to watch).

Secondly, the art of prioritizing, knowing your next action is an art that challenges most teenagers. Allen provides a great framework, what he calls The Four-Criteria Model for Choosing Actions in the Moment. The four criteria look like this:

1. Context- what can I do where I am with the tools I have?
2. Time available- what can I get done before I must stop?
3. Energy available- what can I finish at my current energy level?
4. Priority- given criteria 1-3, what is most important to do?

It's nice to have a set space for getting work done, like a desk that has all of the tools you might need to accomplish your work like a computer, or any books, worksheets, or writing utensils required. But we often find ourselves in places and in situations where we can work but we do not have all our normal resources. Maybe there is no wi-fi, so your Chromebook is useless, or you forgot to put your AP Literature novel in your backpack. This is context, and it is the first criteria to consider.

Time and energy are considered next. Given the amount of time and how you are feeling now, you know what you can accomplish. Students that finish work early in their first period and find themselves with a free thirty minutes are likely to get much more accomplished in that amount of time than students with a found thirty minutes in their final class of the day. Aren't we the same? I know that my morning writing sessions

---

[1] Like those exemplified in the worldwide phenomenon *the life-changing magic of tidying up* by Marie Kondo, who in my opinion is the David Allen of the home.

are much more productive than my after-dinner ones (especially the dinners where a beer or two were had).

Lastly, and maybe most importantly, is priority. It is listed fourth of four simply because the previous three criteria impact what can be done in a way that trumps priority but knowing what needs to be done next and doing it is often hard for students. Imagine your teenager is left alone for a school week, and you have left them five dinners in the fridge knowing that they will get breakfast and lunch at school. It just so happens that each meal has an expiration date that matches each day they need to heat one up for dinner. The expiration dates establish the priority, with each meal to be eaten on the last day it is safe to eat. This makes perfect sense, you have painstakingly explained this to your teenager, and you have left notes attached by magnets to the fridge. Knowing you, you've even left notes on the food that say things like, "eat me first," "eat me on Tuesday," and "save me for last." You and I both know that despite our best efforts, our time away would be cut short because we would receive a call from our teenager as they are being rushed to the hospital for food poisoning. Despite all the warnings, teenagers want to do what they want to do, and that is usually what is the easiest or the most fun.

While I paint an impossible picture that suggests teenagers are incapable of prioritization, they are not, it is just that they struggle with it. Many people do in fact, and it is a sign they failed at this challenge in high school and it is probably led to shortcomings in life. Knowing what to do next, which usually involves an "expiration date," is a skill that takes dogged effort to make a habit. Once date displaces desire though, it will be there forever as a guiding principle.

Found Time

One of the most telling signs of a student that excels and a student that struggles is how they handle found time. Found time is a chunk of time you did not expect to be available to you, and it is an opportunity to utilize Allen's Four-Criteria Model for Choosing Actions in the Moment. High school is going to have lots of found time opportunities—a teacher is absent and doesn't leave the substitute work that completely fills the period, fog or snow creates a one or two hour delay in the start of the school day, an assembly doesn't leave enough time for a teacher to launch into a new assignment so they allow students to work on other classwork—and their habitual response to these moments is very telling.

The very best students are very dutiful in their response. They instantly go to their backpack where their work is kept in a well-organized binder. They quickly assess the context (What can I do with the tools available?), time (How much time until the bell rings?), energy (Which, to be honest, is probably not a question the best students consider. They always have the energy to get work done.), and priority (What do I have that is due next?). After this quick deliberation, they pull out some work and take advantage of the ten to thirty minutes they were just blessed with. They know that this is ten to thirty minutes that they will not need to utilize later in the evening or this weekend. They see school as primarily a place where they get work done, and because they have this mindset, found time moments are easy to take advantage of.

The poorest students see school as mostly a place to socialize and play. Because of this, their reaction to found time is very different. They instantly think, "cool, I can talk to Jake," or "cool, I can play the snake game on my Chromebook." Odds are their backpack is in no condition to allow them to take advantage of this time academically, often resembling a dark corner of a forgotten alley, where windswept debris gathers and coagulates into new forms of matter.

Found time is a precious commodity, and the workers among us know how to take advantage of it.

The Eighth Challenge: PRODUCE

Do Everything Now, Make it Long, and Make it Look Good

Most of the work we do in the world does not receive scrutiny. It may receive a glance, maybe a quick browse, but rarely does someone spend the time to pour over our work with a fine-toothed comb, analyzing our product in detail. School is no different.

We would like to imagine that every assignment a student does in school is thoroughly evaluated by a teacher, with copious markings and in-person feedback given each time. Reality could not be further from the truth. This imagined situation would be impossible to execute beyond a classroom of one. It is also unnecessary. Imagine a basketball coach that stops practice after every shot by every player, evaluating their technique and offering suggestions for improvement. Nothing would ever get accomplished.

Most of what we do in situations where learning is taking place is practice, and practice requires repetitions. Practice demands that sweet spot of quantity and quality, the learner doing as many good reps as possible in the time allotted to improve their skill. In classrooms, this practice will generate a good portion of their grade, as they will do sets of problems, participate in discussions, work in groups to build things, and complete worksheets individually. The product of this practice will receive a glance, like the one you give your neighbor's front yard as you drive to work. In an instant, you can tell whether care was given to the upkeep and maintenance of their plants and grass, or whether it has been neglected, and you need to make an anonymous complaint to the homeowners' association.

Teachers get to know their students quickly through their work. I have about 180 students spread out over six classes, and with 90% or more accuracy I could collect work without names on it and correctly attribute points earned in the gradebook. At the time of this writing, during the Spring Semester, I have spent over half the year looking at their work every day. I know which ones will be done first, which ones will ask for extra time, which ones will try to copy from someone else, and which ones are likely not to do it at all. The teacher-student relationship is unique, complex, and strong.

Most of the work my students turn into me gets a glance. Just as scientists have discovered how much you can know about a person by taking a quick glance of their room[2], I can tell instantly whether a student got what they needed to from the practice. If teachers were not able to work this way, if every piece of work required deep scrutiny, markings, and individual feedback, students would never come close to doing the amount of work necessary to grow.

Knowing this, students need to impress in a glance. Your reaction might be, "wait, shouldn't they focus on doing the assignment and learning what needs to be learned from it?" Yes, but appearances matter, just like the front yard of your neighbor. Making sure the grass survives is not enough. Care must be given to its survival *and* its appearance. If we are shooting for a hero certificate at the end of this journey, these details matter.

The best students make sure their work is done immediately, beyond the length required, and neatly. At a glance, their work always stands out. Just like the front yard you drive past, your glance does not evaluate its appearance in isolation, it does so within the context of all the front yards in the neighborhood. For the best student it is a compulsion that is driven partly by the topic of the next challenge, competition, but also out of a strong connection to their future goals (challenge #3). Doing their best work is a habit.

If every time a student is given work to do their reaction is to start immediately, to utilize all of the space given, and to make the work easily understood and pleasing to the eye, they will get the most out of the practice. If instead they put it off as long as possible, complete each part only to the minimum requirement, and hurriedly compose their responses in a way that appears sloppy, they will get the least out of the practice. It is true that they will get more out of it than the student that

---

[2] Going so far as to suggest we could eliminate so much wasted time getting to know someone on a date if instead each person was just allowed to see the other's bedroom.

does only some of the work or none, but they are still leaving some potential growth on the table. It could be better, and they know it.

Power 20: Work Small for Big Results

I believe in this strategy so much; I am actually working on a book dedicated to this one topic. If every student utilized this strategy, not only would they be much more efficient at getting their schoolwork done, they will have internalized a strategy they can use for the rest of their life for getting *anything* done.

Power 20[3] works by removing the daunting task of a thousand miles and turns it into one step, or more precisely, twenty minutes of steps. It is not a new concept. The most productive people in the world use some version of this strategy to get work done every day. If I sat down to write a book, I would probably never start. I do not even sit down to write a chapter. I write sections, which come together to make chapters, which gather to make a book. It is the idea that one page written a day, which is not an overwhelming task, leads to a 365-page book by the end of the year. Anybody that completes large tasks on a regular basis uses this strategy. Painters tackle a wall at a time, not the whole house. Marathoners keep their focus on the next mile, not all twenty-six. Recovering addicts work to stay clean one day at a time, not their whole life.

The Power 20 has three phases: pre-work, work, and post-work. The objective of the pre-work phase is to get everything ready for the work phase. Gather any necessary materials, clarify any questions about the work to be done, and eliminate any distractions (turn phone off, close out tabs that are open with email or entertainment/game sites). In the

---

[3] Power 20 is a strategy for getting work done that I developed for my students that were struggling to handle large workloads. It is not in any way unique or original, and I read extensively about similar programs while crafting this one, tailoring it to the needs of the population I was working with at the time. Power 20 is the name I gave it, hence the proper capitalization.

pre-work phase, it is also important to establish a post-work reward, like checking social media or having an ice cream sandwich. The benefits of identifying rewards are two-fold: it establishes a carrot to work towards, and it makes work not something you do instead of the fun stuff (denial), but before the fun stuff (delay). Once everything needed to work for twenty minutes is gathered, all distractions are muted, and a reward is identified, it is time to set a timer for twenty minutes and move to the next phase[4].

The work phase is exactly that. Twenty minutes of uninterrupted, non-stop work. Get as much done as possible until the timer goes off. Once it does, it is time to stop.

The post-work phase will either serve as a reward for work finished, or as an intermission between multiple work phases. If it is an intermission, it is good to get up and move around a little, have a non-sugary snack, and maybe even check your phone or email. This should last about three to five minutes, whereupon another Power 20 work session is commenced. Repeat this as often as needed to complete the desired work, or for as long as time allows. Once the work session or sessions are complete, make sure to enjoy a reward and appreciate the amount of work completed.

You might be thinking, *really, just twenty minutes?* You must remember I first started using this strategy with high school freshmen, and twenty minutes was about as long as many of them could be expected to work quietly and independently. Twenty minutes of sustained, uninterrupted work is an awesome feat for many young teenagers. As they become proficient with the strategy, it will naturally expand as their capacity for focused work grows. It is like an exercise routine that goes longer or increases in weight, intensity, or repetitions the stronger you get.

It is also revelatory to them when they finish twenty minutes and realize how much they got done! Young people today are under the delusion they work better with the TV on, or a Netflix show streaming

---

[4] I understand it is most likely a cell phone will be used as the timer. It is best to set it, start it, then place it a distance away where it can still be heard when it goes off, but is out of visual distance to create temptation.

in the background, or their favorite artist blaring in their ears. It is false and flies in the face of all research on the topic. The brain cannot focus on two things at once, and in instances where there is competition for its attention, it spends its time flipping back and forth, and nothing receives its full attention. Quality goes down, mistakes go up, and the time it takes to complete the job increases.

Young people are not only amazed at how much they got done, but also by how good they feel. Many young people never break away from their devices, constantly distracted by music, social media, videos and the like. They have forgotten what it feels like to be clear headed if they ever knew in the first place. They are likely to relapse, but at least they have gotten a taste of it, and hopefully they come back for more. Hopefully, over time they learn how to strike the right balance between work and fun, a challenge they will continue to face for the rest of their lives.

Wrapping It Up

If mentors were polled about which of the ten challenges they most desired their teens to achieve a Ready for Take Off! rating, I believe *Produce* would come out on top. Adults understand that thrust matters, and that getting a strong engine for your vehicle is arguably the most important factor in how far you travel.

At the heart of an engine's power is its brut force ability to be available for duty at the turn of a key. It does not need convincing beyond the request. Turn the key, and it jumps into action. Life rewards workers, especially those that respond like engines do, instantly and with full power.

While an engine's core value is its instant and endless response to do the work asked of it, the volume and quality of that work will be determined by its engineering. Both lawnmower and jet engines are *engines*, but the thrust they provide, and the effort put into crafting them, are quite different. The response to do work is important, but the work they can accomplish will be determined by the complex systems they have installed.

Developing strong organizational systems will be a key determinant of a teenager's ability to produce. Not only can it help declutter the mind to allow them to think more clearly and efficiently, but it is vital for prioritizing and utilizing found time. Integrating systems that produce quality outcomes that are extensive, clean, and stand out from the rest, like that one front yard as you drive through the neighborhood, will help teens receive recognition and advancement. And finally, installing systems that can handle volume, for those times when the work piles up, will not only keep our teenagers from overheating and stalling out entirely, but will keep them humming along (mostly) stress free.

The Challenge's Impact on Trajectories

Ready for Take Off!

Life always rewards the hard worker. The student that develops strong work habits will grow more, do more, be better organized, and continually be moving forward. This is what we want for our children! Remember, this challenge is the jet engine for the plane, and without it, the plane is useless. This is the challenge where potential is either met or squandered. The plane either takes off or sits on the runway while everyone muses, "if that plane only had some engines." This challenge will also play a part in how much a young person develops themself after high school. Education beyond high school is optional, and it is hard. A willingness to commit to the years of hard work necessary to earn advanced skills, be it academically or technically, will take more than desire. Work ethic and strategies to balance work, play, and other responsibilities like a job and maybe a family, takes real skill and drive. Once in the workplace, work ethic and the ability to produce efficient, quality work in quantities desired by the powers that be will be the upward thrust that moves the best workers up the ladder. The difference between getting fired, keeping a job, and moving up the ladder often comes down to work. Mastering this challenge ensures a successful take-off and continued forward motion.

Still Boarding

The consistency in this category are the students that will do the tasks that they enjoy, and this challenge is no different. Adherence to this credo can impact their trajectory in a couple ways, one that sees them flying the middle path, and one that stalls their takeoff altogether. If in fact they do find things in high school they like, and they do develop some skills and some good habits, then a takeoff is possible and maybe they can increase their altitude later. They will not have as broad a skillset as those that work hard at everything, but at least they know what hard work feels like. They will encounter a need to do difficult work that is unpleasant. It is a reality of life, and it will be a fork in the road that will determine how smooth or bumpy the ride is afterwards. The good news is, they're moving, and they'll likely maintain employment and hold their life together if they can plug into a vocation they enjoy and do enough of the unpleasant life tasks, like pay your bills and visit your in-laws. The second group, however, does not even belong in this group.

Flight Delayed

It never fails. Every year I get a significant group of students that belong to the "I only do what I like to do" group, and they conveniently do not like anything about school. This fever dream that they adhere to, that somewhere inside of them is a worker just waiting for the right task, leads them to delusions of teenage grandeur. Every high school teacher will tell you about all of the students that are going to play in the NBA, be a pediatrician (never just a "doctor"), or own their business (and it's almost always just a "business," no specifics given), yet don't even try out for the high school basketball team, hate science, and are terrible at math.

They also lack any work ethic to speak of. It is sad really, because you know in their head that this is a real dream, that they have spent time imagining this future. Dreams make us feel good, but they are only dreams without the energy to make them real. Many students in this group falsely believe they are going to "turn it on" when they want to, that they have access to an internal switch that they will flip to on when the time is right. What they do not realize is that a switch that has been off for too long gets frozen and stuck, and the effort to get it pried loose is greater than they have ever spent in their life, on anything. With no real passion and no real skills, these flights are cancelled until some major changes take place.

PD for Parents & Teachers

For Parents

- Environment plays a huge role in our ability to think and work. The more stable an environment we can provide for our children, with consistent routines for daily activities like eating, sleeping, and bathing, and set spaces for working that reduce distractions and provide the tools necessary to get the job done, the more likely they are to produce.

- A family that works together produces more. If all or most of the family members can commit to getting their work done at the same time, then there is a shared sense of purpose in the act of working. Also, if Junior is doing Geometry proofs at the desk in his bedroom, and hears eruptions of laughter from the living room while the rest of the family is watching Jumanji for the third time, it's unreasonable to think he will be focused. If nobody else has work to do, then enjoy a quiet activity individually and let Junior focus on his work, not what he is missing out on.

- Again, modeling the behaviors you want your children to develop is often our greatest way to influence their choices. How we handle found time, the quality of the work we do, and how we tackle large projects will all be reference points our children access when they encounter similar life moments. The more we can do these out loud, exposing our children to our thought processes, or modeling the use of Power 20 to take advantage of found time, are all powerful ways to teach them how to be good workers.

For Teachers

- Break larger projects and longer assignments into smaller pieces. Instead of having a project with ten components due in two weeks, establish a timeline that has one thing due each day for ten days. They do not need to be collected, just checked, but helping students manage larger assignments by chunking it out will help them finish the project on time. Not doing this increases the likelihood that your less driven students will not do it at all, and even your better students will procrastinate and produce an inferior product.
- Turn "free time" into "found time," a time to be productive. Too often we have students race through their work because they know their teacher will let them play a game on their Chromebook with the time left over in class. Set the standard that class time is dedicated to work, and if they finish an assignment early, they are expected to continue growing as a student. This can be by competing work from another class, reading a choice novel, or even helping other students that are still working and having trouble.
- What we tolerate, we encourage. If you accept sloppy work without a name on it, you send the message that messy and nameless work is ok. Set clear standards for how work should

170

be completed, use models of exemplary work in both appearance and length, and accept nothing less (adjusting, of course, for individual students' abilities). Calmly return work that does not meet the standard and ask for it to be amended. Consistency is the key, and students will get the message and adjust quickly if they hear and the same message again and again.

Habits That Work for Teenagers

- **When a teacher lets me know I have free time, I will check my backpack to see what I can get done in the time available.** By turning the announcement of free (found) time into a trigger to be productive, students will develop that worker mindset that always prioritizes work to be done over fun time.

- **Whenever I am given information about assignment due dates or upcoming exams, I will write it down in my planner.** The organized worker is the best worker. Not only does this help ensure work is done on time, but by offloading this information from the brain into a safe and secure location (the planner), the student's ability to think is clearer and more efficient.

- **Whenever I am given an assignment, I will immediately get to work on making it as complete and neat as I possibly can.** This is the habit of all of the best students, while the others react to assignments with thoughts like, "How long can I put this off?", "How little can I do and still receive credit?", and "How messy can it be before the teacher gives me heck?" Not only do all these reactions to work produce inferior products, they add time to completion. The best workers not only do the longest and best-looking work, they are the first one done because they did not waste time trying to not do the assignment or trying to do a lesser version.

Chapter Nine

The Ninth Challenge:
COMPETE

My dear fellow, it isn't easy to be anything nowadays. There's such a lot of beastly competition about.

From *The Importance of Being Earnest* by Oscar Wilde

In his book *The Power of Habit: Why We Do What We Do in Life and Business*, Charles Duhigg posits that, "Companies aren't families. They're battlefields in a civil war." This succinct and rather brutal statement hints at why the ninth challenge is a vital part of the quest.

But it only speaks to half of the challenge's value. Yes, the world is a competitive place, and to ignore this fact is to commit to the life of a shut-in, and a broke and single one at that. We are constantly competing for jobs, a spot on the team, a parking spot, tickets to a concert, an attractive partner, a raise, customers, and attention. Every day we wake up and begin a day that will see us participate in many competitive situations, and the outcomes of those situations hinge on our readiness for battle.

Just being good at competition is not reason enough for the challenge to be an integral part of the high school experience. It is important because when we compete, we improve. Nothing sharpens our focus and effort to improve like impending competition, and nothing informs us of our progress better than its results. We learn a lot when we compete: how we stack up against others, whether our methods of preparation were effective, what our strengths are, and what our weaknesses are. It is also good at letting us know whether this game is for us, and whether we should continue in our pursuit or travel another path.

The exalted among us, those humans that have made the greatest impact on this planet, were excellent at this challenge. They embraced it as a tool for intense improvement, and they used advanced strategies and fortitude to win much more than they lost. Even their losses were victories, serving as teachers and fuel. It could be argued that without this challenge, if somehow the world were suddenly stripped of competition, we would still be hunched over and grunting. It was competition between the USA and Russia that got us to the moon, and it will be competition that delivers us to the deeper reaches of the universe.

Competition can have a dark side too. It can drive people to cheat, it can end relationships, and it can cause emotional distress. It is like fire: when used properly it makes our food edible and our steel strong, while misuse can destroy communities and take lives. It is important to have a healthy respect for competition, to take the time to understand its benefits, its drawbacks, and how to use it wisely.

Students in high school are going to encounter a lot of competition. Beyond the obvious of athletics, just about every facet of high school life will involve a level of challenge. Bands will compete for best in show, students will run against each other for student council positions, valedictorians will vie for best overall GPA, groups of friends will jostle for the best table in the cafeteria, football players will fight for the attention of the cheer captain, seniors will rev their engines for parking lot supremacy, and the teacher's pets will be scrambling for the best seats in the front row.

And in the primary measurement of high school, their performance in the classroom, there take place the Tour de France of competitions, the class rank. After each semester, student's report cards will indicate their place in the race, where they landed in comparison to every other student in their grade. When put up against everyone else that's generally the same age, that has generally the same experience with school, that is taking mostly the same classes, and that lives in the same general area, where do they fit in? Outside of the smallest schools, this will likely be a comparison to hundreds of other teenagers, all of them facing the ten challenges together.

Classroom Grades & Class Rank

One of the greatest advances when we moved over from manually keeping and computing grades with pencil and paper to entering scores into a computer to calculate, was the ability to run myriad reports based on the entered data. Once you have entered how students did on one or more assignments, a project, and some quizzes and tests, a teacher can now go into the computer and ask it to produce reports based on that input. These reports can supply information on the whole class, like how they did on a test and whether or not reteaching is needed or they're ready to move on, or they can be individual student reports that show their progress and any assignments they're missing and need to make up. Reports can even be based on data beyond the classroom, like on a student's attendance, behavior, or performance in other classrooms, as the system that teachers are inputting classroom level scores into is likely the system that collects *all* student information. When a counselor sits down with a student, all they need to do is pull up a student's profile to see how they are doing academically, their attendance, and any behavioral issues they have had. If they need to contact home, all that information is there as well. Now that I think about it, these kids are screwed! Just twenty years ago this information was likely held in ten different places, much of it kept by hand, and getting a full picture of a student was a difficult task that required quite a bit of effort to accumulate. Kind of like how advances in DNA testing have made it more difficult for criminals to get away with it, students too are under a more intense microscope.

One of a classroom teacher's favorite reports to run, however, is the class progress report, which simply spits out a snapshot of what is going on in the gradebook system. To protect their identities, the report is run using student identification numbers instead of names, and it shows all the assignments and the scores received for each assignment, and what grade each student has currently in the class. These can be printed and posted in the classroom for students to look at and see their progress.

Right about now you are probably thinking to yourself that this is an unnecessary action. As described in the embrace criticism chapter, students now have access to this information directly and should be checking it daily, so why does a teacher need to print it out for them to see? While this is true, the limitation is that they can only see their progress; they have no idea how they are stacking up against others. Teachers are likely, when they run these reports, manipulating the information so that it is organized by overall grade, not by alphabet or student identification number (this is also another way to protect identity). The computer will organize the information so that the student with the highest percentage appears at the top, and everyone else will appear in descending order beneath them.

The extreme value of this report is context. A grade of "A" is impressive, but less so if everyone has one. A grade of "C+" may be disappointing, but when it is the third highest grade in a class of 35, it takes on new meaning. Knowing how we are doing by ourselves against a set of standards is good but knowing how our progress stands up against others approaching the same standards, at the same time, from the same instructor, is invaluable. This is one of the great benefits of competition: how am I doing in comparison to others?

I know, I know, again you are asking, "doesn't all comparison lead to misery?" Yes, it can, if it becomes an obsessive pursuit and a zealousness to come out on top develops into a win at all costs mentality. If the focus turns to winning instead of growing, then the participant's relationship with competition has eroded into an unhealthy one. If the focus remains on using this feedback for growth, to take stock of what is working, what isn't, and what those above are doing that we aren't, then a healthy relationship with competition can be maintained and progress can be made.

At the end of the semester, when grades are submitted by teachers and report cards are generated, there will likely be class rank information. It will look something like this:

Class Rank: 56 out of 412

What does this tell us? First, this information is based solely on the semester this report was generated for[1]. What the "56" tells us is that 55 students performed better this semester than they did. Their grades produced a higher GPA. The "412" tells us that there were 412 students in the same grade and at the same school that earned grades that semester. So, if you do the math, about 356 students had a lower GPA. The reason I say about, is that it is unlikely that each of the 412 students had a unique GPA, in fact it is impossible. With only so many grades and so many classes, only so many GPAs can be generated. In the case of our example, it might have worked out something like this:

---

[1] Your student's report card may also include a section where "Cumulative GPA" appears, which indicates their progress in all their classes in high school to this point. There may also appear a class rank based on cumulative GPA, which is how valedictorians—student #1 after four years—and salutatorians—student #2 after four years—are determined. In my district, valedictorian has come to mean "anyone with a cumulative GPA of 4.0 or better," which creates a group of valedictorians, and the single salutatorian is the student with the next highest cumulative GPA that was not a 4.0. Poor kid. My heart goes out to them when they are announced each year at graduation in front of a football stadium full of parents and friends, essentially saying, "and this student got as close as you could get to being a valedictorian, but because they bombed that one test in algebra their freshman year, they're not."

- 27 students earned a 4.0. They are all ranked as "1 out of 412" because they all tied for first with the same GPA consisting of all As.
- 28 students earned the next highest GPA of 3.8. They are all ranked as "28 out of 412" because 27 students had higher GPAs than them.
- 17 students earned the next highest GPA of 3.6. They are all ranked "56 out 412" because 55 students (27 with a 4.0 + 28 with a 3.8) had higher GPAs than them.
- And so on

So, while the student that is ranked 56 out of 412 can be assured that 55 students fared better GPA-wise this semester, they likely shared this position with a group of students. This also means that the unfortunate group at the bottom with the worst GPA will share their position, meaning nobody has the unfortunate rank of "412 out of 412." I doubt this group cares about class rank anyway.

All these reports, from the classroom grade report that ranks performance within a class, to the class rank that appears on a report card and shows how a student compares to everyone else in their grade, have value. Their critical feedback[2] provides context, allowing the earner to get a deeper understanding of what their grade and GPA means. It also provides motivation to those that have a healthy relationship with the power of competition to make them better.

Preparation for Competition as Antidote to Anxiety

Imagine you have scored tickets to the Super Bowl! You won a radio call-in contest, and you and another person of your choosing have received an all-expenses paid trip to one of the most watched events in the world.

---

[2] I imagine you have caught on to the fact that *compete* and *embrace criticism* are challenges that are intimately linked.

Two tickets on the 50-yard line! You are at the venue, and you got there as early as you could to take in all the hoopla. You have just settled into your seat, beer in one hand and hot dog in the other, and you watch these magnificent athletes warm-up. These two teams have spent the past year practicing, learning, playing, studying, and growing. They have spent most of their lives preparing their body and mind for this moment. The electricity in the air has everyone so pumped to be a part of this special day! Then you notice the head coach from one of the teams leave the field and enter the stands. He starts walking up the aisle, and the fans are mesmerized. He stops as he gets to your row, looks around, and then makes a bee line towards you. He pauses as he gets to your seat and asks, "Have you ever played quarterback?"

To which you answer, quite shaken, "Yes, a little bit. In high school."

"We need you to suit up," he says quite seriously, "all of our quarterbacks are in the hospital with a bad flu. We need you to fill in."

How you might be feeling, as you walk onto the field with your helmet on, partially digested hot dog and beer in your belly, is how many of our students often feel at school. You're about to get your lunch handed to you by men that have worked way harder than you, in a game you didn't prepare for, in a sport you haven't participated in for over a decade. To make it even worse, millions of people are going to watch it happen.

There is a yucky feeling we get when we show up for something unprepared, and it is worse when the lack of preparation was a choice we made. Most of life's bigger moments are known to us in advance, like when we need to prepare a year-end report for the board of directors, give a speech at our friend's wedding, or get the house ready for a big family gathering. If we fail to prepare for these moments, instead choosing to wing it, not only do we have zero chance of doing our best, but we are likely going to experience some anxiety. The more we do this to ourselves, the more anxious we become.

I remember being at a parent conference for my son when he was a freshman and struggling with algebra. The teacher displayed the tests he had taken and done poorly on, and his counselor, who was also present, looked at my son and suggested he was suffering from "test anxiety." He then launched into a joke filled story about his issues with test anxiety and how he sometimes needed to breathe into a paper bag to calm himself down, miming the act with an invisible paper bag. It took everything I had to not lunge across the table, shove the imaginary bag down his throat, and throttle his neck. Instead, I calmly negated this ridiculous suggestion and instead got back to the real cause of my son's poor performance: failure to prepare. Thankfully, my son is not prone to feelings of anxiety (ambivalence, maybe), but the rise of anxiety as a reason why we cannot perform to our peak ability is frustrating as a teacher and parent. As a matter of self-preservation, this can often lead to adoption of the "I'm just not good at this" mantra that relieves people entirely of the need to prepare or feel anxious.

I am aware that my grandpa slippers are on at the moment, and I am aware that anxiety is a real thing that real people suffer from and need real help to deal with, but sometimes there's real truth in what grandpa says, no matter how old school it sounds. Here goes:

For many students, test anxiety is an excuse to not prepare.

Do kids get nervous? Sure, they do. Sometimes the stakes are high, and they are afraid they will not perform as well as they need to. But the level of their nervousness is likely proportional to their level of preparation. It's dependent upon how well they paid attention in class, whether or not they met with their teacher to clarify questions they had, how thoroughly they approached their homework, how much exam specific studying they did, and whether or not they accessed any tutoring opportunities.

Students will often say, "I'm bad at math." But you never hear them say, "I'm bad at Minecraft," or "I really suck at Snapchat," or, "I'm just not that good at eating hot chips." Why not? Because they do those activities *all the time*. They are prepared for them. Do any of them ever complain of video game anxiety? No, they do not.

I know I am treading clumsily into a touchy subject, and it may sound like I am dismissing anxiety as a real condition that people suffer from. I am not, or at least I hope I am not, and I apologize if it is taken that way. I just do not like the trend I am seeing of anxiety as a reason for poor performance when the real culprit is failure to prepare. It is extra frustrating when this self-imposed anxiety results in the sufferer taking it a step further and announcing that they are just not good at the activity. It is just not true.

If we can get them to say, "I'm bad at preparing," and then get them to prepare for big moments they know are coming, then we can start moving forward.

Reading the Cards

I graduated high school in 1987, and while I was there the board game Trivial Pursuit was huge. Almost every household had their own copy, and everyone was playing it at social gatherings. Even fast food restaurants were doing Trivial Pursuit cross promotions, with customers getting a chance to play when they bought a burger meal. My high school was caught up in the frenzy and decided to have a lunchtime Trivial Pursuit tournament. I joined a team and we entered.

It just so happened that my family owned a copy of Trivial Pursuit, the classic version that was going to be used in the tournament. Knowing that each copy of Trivial Pursuit had the same box of question cards with the answers on them, I went to the closet where the game was stored and grabbed the box of questions *and answer* cards. For about a week prior to the tournament, I sat and read the cards. I probably read each card a few times.

Now I fully acknowledge that I, if I were a teenager today, would probably not have spent my time reading the Trivial Pursuit cards in my spare time. I most likely would have binged Netflix, played Fortnite, scanned Snapchat, or indulged in any of the other distractions teens face today. But in the 1980s, I did not have those things, so I read the cards.

When the tournament came, I was dominant. I was not surprised by a single question, and I remembered almost all of them that were asked (I will admit I have an abnormally strong ability to memorize and recall facts).

In my mind, I did not cheat. I prepared. I knew what I was going to be tested on and I took the time to digest it.

Just like every situation students are going to encounter in school, they have access to all the answers prior to them being asked. They do homework, they engage in conversations, they take notes, they read from books, and they do online activities. They are given access to the cards.

Read the cards!

The Workplace Game

Schools, for the most part, are stuck with students. Students can fail to do their work, or do poor quality work, and they can even have higher than average absences, but while there are some consequences like bad grades or lunch detention, schools are still going to let them in the door. We want them to change those bad habits into good ones, and we are going to offer lots of support and tons of resources to help them get there. But that scenario is about to change.

Act that way at a job and they will be fired. Get fired from multiple jobs, and good luck trying to get another. They better hope their parents are cool with them living in their bedroom for a long time, as in forever.

Students should play this mental game in every class they have in high school:

Imagine the class is a company—a factory, an office, whatever. The teacher is the boss, owner, President, Big Cheese, the decision maker. All the students are the employees, the workers.

The semester is the trial period when all the workers are on probation. This is a common workplace practice, where businesses evaluate their new employees over the first 3-6 months on the job to determine whether they want to keep them around. So, imagine the first semester is this probationary period, and at the end of it the boss (teacher) is going to make these determinations:

- The top 10% of the workers (students) are going to be promoted to a management training program. They will receive raises and will be the future managers and supervisors of the company. In a class of 30, this would be 3 students.

- All students that earned a D or F are being fired. The company cannot afford to keep workers around that fail to do even average work. They will be replaced with new recruits.

- Anyone absent 10% or more of the days, regardless of final grade is also fired. Companies have a hard time functioning when their employees do not show up regularly. Attendance is prized in the workplace. In a semester, this would be about ten or more days absent.

- Most students with Cs and Bs will be retained and will comprise most of the workforce. The C students may not receive raises and may be told that their probationary time is being extended and their work needs to be improved. The B students will receive small raises, but a leadership position is not currently seen for them.

- The A students not promoted to the Management Training Program will receive larger raises and depending how they continue to improve may be promoted to management sometime in the future. They may also be afforded priority choice when it comes to shifts or areas to work within the company. This could mean the more lucrative shifts, like a Saturday night at a restaurant when there is more customers and the tips earned are greater.

At the end of the semester, they could look at the reports generated that tell them how they did in comparison to their classmates. They can then ask themselves, "Am I good with this scenario?" or maybe, "Does this match how I want my life to turn out?" If the answer is yes, then they are on the right track. Their habits are producing the results they desire. Their trajectory matches their goals.

If the answer is no, it is time for some serious reflection and some behavior changes before next semester. Luckily, this is not a single-elimination tournament. There are eight semesters in four years. That is eight opportunities to play, reflect, learn, and improve.

The "A" Students Have the Most Fun

Unfortunately, it is a popular notion that the "bad" students are having the most fun. They are not doing anything they do not want to. They are not doing homework, showing up on time, or paying attention during lectures. They are always laughing, and they have this devil may care freedom as they get sent up to the office yet again. They are always just hanging out in a hallway somewhere while everyone else is slaving away over algebra. How could they get so lucky?

It may seem like they are having the most fun, and I know there are many times the more disciplined students wish they could hang out in a hallway instead of working on an in-class essay. They should not be deceived, however, even if some of the great movies about high school, including one of my favorites *Say Anything*, play on this theme. In it, the beautiful high school valedictorian played by Ione Skye reflects on her conservative high school life and laments not doing anything she should not have, leading to a summer fling with John Cusack, a marginal graduate who is into kickboxing.

The truth is the "bad" kids are "enjoying" empty fun. It is thin and evaporates quickly. Sitting on the curb at the local Gas-n-Sip, eating chips, drinking beer and espousing "wisdom" about women, does not lead to anything. It's a great scene in *Say Anything* when John Cusack realizes this and challenges the boys engaging in this activity that if they know so much about women, why are they sitting here at a Gas-n-Sip at night without a girl in sight.

After a moment of silence, they all respond, "by choice, man."

Sure. And I bet they all suffer from test anxiety, too.

Meanwhile, the happiest kids on campus, and by happy, I mean a deep, powerful, thick and lasting joy, are the A students. They make different choices.

But how? They are always doing work, right? How do they have time for fun?

Have you ever tried your best, at anything? Have you ever accomplished something that was challenging? Have you ever earned something few others have? Have you ever had people you respect praise your effort and accomplishments? Have you ever gone out and enjoyed yourself knowing EVERYTHING you are supposed to do is complete, and to a high quality?

If you answered no to all these questions, we have some work to do. The truth is, having just one of those things happen feels amazing, and the A students are having them all happen, all the time.

So, the next time your student is hanging with their friends, playing video games, or maybe at the mall, and they have that small, nagging pit in their stomach that is their algebra homework or the vocabulary test they have tomorrow that they haven't prepared for, ask them what it would feel like if it was done. What if they were fully, totally, and confidently ready for everything they had tomorrow?

Think they might, in a deep and thorough way, really enjoy the moment in a way they are not used to? Think they might feel a joy greater than anything they have felt before?

If they are not sure, encourage them to ask the "A" kids.

Just make sure they do not seek advice from the crew sitting on the curb at Gas-n-Sip.

The Added Value of High School Sports

Sports are such a ubiquitous part of not just American culture, but the culture of the world, that sometimes it is hard to think about them objectively, but let us give it a shot. Think about all the money, land, resources, and time dedicated to playing what are essentially games. These games have no impact on things that really matter, like who the president is, what the price of oil is, or what the next new flavor of Coke will be. They are, when you get down to it, games.

But if you search for a high school on a map and you choose "satellite view," you are most likely going to see that most of a high school's acreage is dedicated to athletic fields. While it's not the majority of a school district's budget, when you take into account the facilities, their upkeep, uniforms, equipment, transportation, staffing (coaching, ticket takers, locker room attendants, referees, etc.), tournament entry fees, and all of the other costs associated with high school athletics, it's amazing how much of a school district's resources are dedicated to an *optional* activity. It is even more amazing when you consider whatever revenue is generated does not come close to outweighing the costs, and that maybe 1% of the athletes on the average high school campus will continue to play sports in college. Even fewer than that will become professional athletes! So why do we do it? If we are committing all these resources so that 1/100th of 1% can play sports for a living, we are not very good at allocating resources where it matters.

It is obviously not about creating opportunities for students to make a living as a professional athlete, especially considering that so many sports do not even have a professional level.

Sports replicate life. They teach us about teamwork, the value of preparation, delayed gratification, handling stressful situations, how to be humble in victory and gracious in defeat. We learn that the right level of challenge keeps us engaged, while work that is too easy is boring, and too difficult is exhausting.

When the softball player steps up to bat, all eyes are on her, and she is either going to get on base or be out. It is her against the pitcher. Who can handle the stress better? Who prepared better?

Moments like this happen again and again in sports. Sports are not a panacea, but they are one of the best ways we know as a society to grow important life skills in our children as evidenced by how we dedicate our resources.

There are other ways, through artistic pursuits like dance, or academic pursuits like the growing field of robotics competitions. Spelling Bees and chess competitions start at young ages. Learning an instrument can also lead to competitive situations.

Whether it is through sports or some other pursuit, it should be obvious that our society has embraced competition, and it has worked out well.

Wrapping It Up

Carol Dweck and her work on identifying the growth mindset, has had a major influence on education and many other fields since her book *Mindset: The New Psychology of Success* was first published in 2006. She found that there are two mindsets, a growth and a fixed mindset. Those with a growth mindset believe that they can improve through effort, while those with a fixed mindset imagine themselves to be largely set in their abilities. They shy away from activities that are difficult because the difficulty is a signal that this must be outside of their predetermined wheelhouse.

One of the qualities that a growth mindset person has is that they are inspired by the success of others. Conversely, the fixed mindset person is threatened when others enjoy success. It is this distinction that may be at the heart of whether someone enjoys a healthy or unhealthy relationship with competition.

The idea of sportsmanship is important in athletics. We should engage with our competitor honestly and earnestly, and we should value their doing the same. Our competitors inspire us to be better, because without them, our efforts would be meaningless. They give us purpose, they push us, and they provide a powerful mirror for our reflection.

Every part of our world is competitive. The animal kingdom is a continuous battle for food, territory, mates, and even sunlight as plants on the forest floor reach skyward to break through the canopy. While we, humans, are more civilized, more developed, we are no less competitive. It drives our economy and is an important pillar of our culture. It is also, at least in America, why we tend to be leery of more socialized forms of government. We fear it will be the end of competition and the innovation it inspires.

The Challenge's Impact on Trajectories

Ready for Take Off!

These students have embraced competition as a tool to improve. They engage in activities that involve competition, and they find ways to insert it into situations that do not formally have it because they understand its power to motivate. Their desire to win inspires them to prepare for competitive situations, so they will not just "wing it" when it comes to important moments like job interviews. They also do not limit themselves to only situations they feel they can win, having experienced defeat in high school and accepting it as a very important part of the competitive process. Because of it, they are willing to seize opportunities others shy away from, understanding that even if they do not get it, they will learn and grow from the experience and be that much closer to getting it next time. While others plateau or stall altogether, their competitive drive keeps them moving forward and upward, and it keeps them engaged in a meaningful life.

Still Boarding

Like my student Eddie from a previous chapter, students here have not learned how to apply their competitive skills outside of sports or other areas of interest. Like Eddie, once they apply their skills beyond areas of comfort and into areas they avoid, they will see their trajectory change, and with it their enjoyment of activities they previously disliked will improve. They may even find new interests to pursue. Another potential reason for their stall may be how they are processing competition. They may care more about winning than improving, which can lead to them only doing activities they can easily win. It can also lead to them taking shortcuts or cheating, putting their character at risk and requiring some rehabilitation when they are found out.

Flight Delayed

Most likely adopting the "I hate competition" stance, this group has embraced a philosophy that allows them to skip out on most of life. Like the group of boys sitting on the curb of the Gas-n-Sip talking about girls instead of competing for their attention, they excuse their forfeit as "choice, man." Competition has expectations that its participants prepare for and grapple with difficult situations. It also introduces the possibility of being labeled a loser, a title nobody wants. These aspects of competition—the work, the struggle, the possibility of losing—have prevented this group from participating in life itself. Instead, they sit on a curb by choice and talk about how lame everyone else is that chose to compete. How convenient.

PD for Parents & Teachers

For Parents

- Expectations are important, but *realistic* expectations even more so. Make sure the expectations you have for your child can be met. They do not have to be easily met, but with reasonable effort and the proper amount of support, success is achievable. Unrealistic expectations can lead to real stress and anxiety, and real friction in your relationship with your teen.
- When report cards come out, have a low stake and non-judgmental conversation with your child about "class rank." Ask

questions like, "What can you learn from those ranked higher?" and, "What did you do better than those ranked behind you?" See it as an opportunity to develop a healthy relationship with competition and how it can help us improve by emulating the behaviors of those that are currently performing at a higher level.

- Use competition in a healthy way within your family. Create challenges that are beneficial and doable, like "who can make their bed every day before school for a month?" With competition like this, anyone that meets the challenge wins, and good habits are developed. Make it a point to show how competition was used to improve behavior and provide motivation.

For Teachers

- Use whole class progress reports to highlight what is creating the hierarchy of performance. Making sure to obscure any information that reveals student identity, point out that as the report moves from top to bottom, there are more blanks indicating work not completed, and less preparation has led to lower exam scores. Want to move up? Do the work and study for tests. The reports make this clear and visible.

- Help students prepare for exams! Use study guides to focus their preparation, teach study techniques and commit class time to it, and find a way to make studying an assignment, where points will be assigned. Students are much more likely to do something they are expected to do and given the time to do it. Do not complain that "students don't study!" Teach them how!

- When using competition in the classroom, be aware of how individual students respond. Help the overzealous competitors chill, and the avoidant to step up. Technology and the "gamification" of just about everything imaginable in education has led to an abundance of competition in today's classrooms. Instead of blindly rolling these activities out, take stock of how your students respond and adjust accordingly.

Habits That Work for Teenagers

- **When I have a test coming up, I will dedicate at least 15 minutes a night for four consecutive nights to studying.** By dedicating one hour to preparation and doing so in a manner that is more effective (fifteen minutes over four nights versus a one hour cram the night before), students are taking ownership of their preparation for serious events.

- **In every class that I have, I will try to be one of the top five students in the class.** By setting personal goals that include competition, students are learning how to self-motivate. This act also ignites their powers of observation, as they are more likely to be aware of how other top students are behaving and then adopting similar characteristics.

- **Prior to each exam, I will take a deep, calming breath and remind myself of all the preparation I did.** Not only does preparation for important moments increase our ability to perform at our best, it can also serve to relax and focus us prior to its beginning. A relaxed mind is open and accessible, while a stressed mind can be closed, making it difficult to find the information that got filed away during study time.

Chapter Ten

The Tenth Challenge:
HANDLE RESPONSIBILITY

Liberty means responsibility. That is why most men dread it.

From *Man and Superman* by George Bernard Shaw

We end here purposefully.

In his enlightening book *Failure to Launch*, clinical psychologist Dr. Mark McConville states plainly that, "If we needed a one-word definition of what it means to be a grown-up, an adult, that one word would be *responsibility*." He goes on to say that, "Not surprisingly, the most common presenting issue I hear about when meeting with struggling transitioners and their parents is mis- or under-management of responsibilities."

It is easy for us to forget how massive and intimidating the transition from high school into the world is. For me, that was over thirty years ago, and I've been adulting so long and am so well versed in the language and culture of being an adult that I lose sight of how harrowing it can be for a teenager in their senior year of high school. What is the big deal? It is so easy! *And I am someone that works at a high school and whose job is to help teenagers mature into functioning adults*! Things we take for granted, like setting up utilities at a new residence, applying for a car loan, and scheduling a plumber to take a look at a leaky pipe are all actions we take for granted because we've done them multiple times, and we've probably been doing them for many years.

But what was it like that first time?

While teenagers will always dream about a liberated future, one where they finally break free of the oppressive restrictions placed upon them by their parents and other adults, as that day draws nearer and all of the impending responsibilities become clearer, their single bedroom, which comes with free wi-fi and a stocked fridge down the hall, all of sudden doesn't seem so…oppressive. Their life to this point has been largely managed by adults, with everything from what to do when they are sick, to paying for car registration, to even when and where to study being a mandate pushed down from above. Outside of which Netflix series to binge next[1], teenagers have not had to deal much with managing their lives. They stand at the edge of a very steep cliff looking out at an endless sea of blue, where all of the support that made their childhood so comfortable, support that they're just now starting to understand and appreciate, is about to disappear and they'll be shoved into a freefall toward the vast ocean of adulthood. Is it going to hurt when I hit the surface? What creatures live out there? What if I have trouble swimming? At least that is how they perceive it, and their perception is their reality.

Our job as adults that are parenting and teaching teenagers is to take that steep cliff and turn it into a gently sloping beach. It is much easier to enter the water from the shoreline, where the land and ocean meet. At the water's edge, both the land and ocean are equal, and as you walk into the water the land beneath your feet slowly gives way, as more and more of your body becomes submerged. It feels safe, and you control the descent at a pace that you feel comfortable with, allowing more and more of your body to acclimate to this new temperature, to this new buoyancy. You can look down into the water and see your feet, legs, and torso through the surface, slightly distorted but still recognizably yours. You move your arms through this new substance and its increased resistance.

---

[1] Surprisingly, even this decision seems to paralyze many teenagers, who instead choose to watch the same series over and over!

Eventually you are ready for full submersion and push your feet off the earth and begin to move your body in new ways, the new ways demanded by your new surroundings and their new rules of behavior and movement. Once in, you pop up to the surface and look back at the shore and realize how far out you are. You remember any trepidation you had and tease yourself for being unsure. It feels good out here! What was I so afraid of? Then you turn, confidently, towards the horizon and marvel at the vastness and beauty of the ocean.

If you have been to a beach on a crowded summer day, you know this process is different for everyone that dares it. For many it is a slow process like the one I just described, involving many long pauses for temperature acclimation. For others, the process is wild and reckless as they run down the beach and hurtle themselves into the oncoming waves. Each teenager will have their own way of entering the water and we need to respect that. Our goal is to make sure they do not avoid the ocean altogether, choosing instead to spend the whole day lying on their towel and playing on their phone.

This challenge, more than any of the others, will deal with a teenager's life inside *and* outside of high school. It is this challenge where we start to see a blending of the safe and familiar confines of school and home with the surrounding world. During this period of transition, students can start to drive themselves to soccer practice, manage an allowance that makes sure they have enough for food *and* gas, and get that first job that will demand greater time management. School will continue with its familiar requirements for responsible behavior, namely doing all their assignments and studying for all their tests, but these demands will increasingly find themselves competing for attention. As our teenagers progress through high school, their life will begin to take on a complexity that is new to them. Their social lives will grow, their work responsibilities will grow, and their academic expectations will grow. All of this means one thing: their capacity for handling responsibilities *must grow*.

The Best Class I Ever Took

I was a theatre arts major in college. I did not start out as one, meandering through majors with mild interest until taking an Acting for Non-Majors course to fulfill a general education requirement. I was instantly hooked and marched down to the administration building to add another layer of whiteout to my declaration of major form.

At California State University, Long Beach (Go Beach!), all theatre majors were required to take a course called *Showcase*, which met once a week on Fridays at noon. Every Friday we piled into a long, rectangular, wooden floored room where some of our acting, directing, and movement classes were held. There were no seats, so like elementary students at an assembly, we flopped onto the floor. The "class" would start with some general announcements about upcoming auditions or other theatre department business, but it would quickly be turned over to the real reason we were all there: to watch a student production.

At the beginning of each semester, individuals or groups of students would submit proposals to be granted one of the Fridays for their production. Faculty would review the proposals and set a calendar. Participating in any of the productions was entirely optional. The only requirement was to be enrolled and show up and be in the audience.

Competition for one of the twelve or so Friday production slots was fierce! The proposals ran the gamut from classic scripts to original pieces, comedy to drama, one person shows to large ensembles. Some proposals were fully formed, with the director, support crew, and entire cast already assembled. Others were the vision of a single person that would hold auditions and assemble a crew once they were selected.

Once the calendar was set, all of those that had their proposals selected went to work. A rehearsal schedule needed to be made considering all cast members busy schedules[2], and rehearsal space needed

---

[2] Everyone involved had jobs, other classes, and were in the department's main stage productions that required twenty plus hours a week of rehearsal, so scheduling rehearsal time for Showcase productions was a huge project.

to be found. Costumes needed to be gathered, a soundtrack made, and props constructed. The week prior to their performance, groups would get into the performance space to dial in the lighting, arrange the rudimentary stage furniture, and run the show again, and again, and again. Rehearsals would routinely run into the wee hours. Everyone involved knew they were about to get one shot to impress the most critical audience of all, their peers.

And they did this by choice without a teacher in sight. It was a pass/fail class, and everyone passed, whether you sat in the audience all semester or were involved in one or more productions[3].

I remember my first year in the department, sitting near the back of the room and watching in awe each Friday as students, with much more talent and experience than I had got up there weekly and bared their souls. Some Fridays I walked away feeling that I had made a mistake, that there was no way I was ever going to get a role if I had to audition against talent like this. Other Fridays it was an uncomfortable hour of cringing, of wondering why someone, somewhere did not stop this train wreck before it got this far. But over time, as I got comfortable in the department and started to make friends, I desperately wanted to be a part of it. I wanted to be up there.

After that first year I made it a point to get involved with as many Showcase productions as possible, and it was the greatest preparation for life I ever went through. Every one of the ten challenges were involved when you were selected to be a part of production—managing your health to keep your energy up, exercising willpower to make sacrifices, having a strong vision of the finished product, understanding the system to earn slot and gather the needed resources, taking feedback from the

---

[3] As you can probably imagine, the students that were the most active in Showcase were also the most successful in the department. When you went to watch a mainstage production that was directed by faculty and staged in the department's large theater with the full weight of the department behind it, the students that were earning these plum roles were also the ones you saw most often on Fridays at noon. Those that only sat in the audience got good at sitting in the audience.

director to improve your performance, embracing the challenge of mounting a complex production, learning lines and blocking (the actor's movements on stage), producing an hour's worth of entertaining theatre, competing with other actors for roles and other productions for a spot on the calendar, and being 100% responsible for *everything*.

Outside of faculty receiving the proposals and determining the calendar, they were not involved in the process at all. Some of them were present at the Showcase, and they may or may not offer some curt feedback, but this was all about the students.

And because of all of that, it was the best class I ever took.

The "Showcases" of High School

It was during reflection, years later, when I realized what my Showcase experience meant to my development. At that time, I was just a pumped theatre student throwing himself headfirst into a new adventure. But as I do with just about everything I learn and find out to be a beneficial life accelerator, I ask myself, "How can this be applied to high school students?"

As I started looking around, I realized it was already being applied. There are many school-based opportunities for students to take on a leadership role and be responsible for a project, a group, or an event, reaping similar benefits that I gained from Showcase, namely handling responsibility.

A hat that I have been wearing for the last five years is yearbook adviser, where I oversee the production of our school's annual yearbook. I usually have a modest staff of about fifteen students, a mix of new and returning staffers, and each year these students produce a 200-page yearbook. I intervene as little as possible, mostly to ensure financial integrity and that deadlines are met, but by and large those fifteen staffers coordinate the coverage of a yearlong series of events and organizations, documenting it all in a historical, primary document. They manage equipment, communicate with coaches and club advisers to coordinate pictures, interview students, design layouts, upload pictures, compose text, and sell and distribute hundreds of yearbooks. I was not involved with yearbook as a student, but as soon as I took it on and learned what it was all about, I suggested that my middle school daughter get involved with her middle school yearbook. She is done it the last two years and will join my staff next year.

What I did do in high school was student government. Known by many names[4]—ASB (Associated Student Body), Student Council, and Class Council to name a few—these groups can often include a mix of elected and non-elected student volunteers and are a great opportunity to take on responsibility. These groups routinely put on events like Homecoming, dances, and all-school rallies. They make decorations, set-up of the venue, work shifts, act as emcee, and clean up afterwards. Getting involved with leadership groups is a great way to experience the responsibility of planning, creating, and hosting events.

While student government groups are usually responsible for many events during the school year, there are many smaller organizations, called clubs, that may host a signature event annually. Dances, poetry nights, or movie night fundraisers are events that clubs may spend weeks planning, organizing and hosting to raise funds or promote their interests. It is on high school campuses where clubs truly come alive, gathering groups of likeminded students around a common faith or culture, or special interests like Anime or music. Academic clubs thrive too, with groups like Robotics, Academic Decathlon, or Mock Trial organizing and training students to compete against groups from other schools.

Leadership positions within groups led by adults, like being a captain of a sports team or a drum major in the band, is another way to assume a mantle of responsibility. Adults lean on their student leaders to promote a positive team culture, to lead their peers in drills, and to corral

---

[4] I went to Westminster High School in Westminster, California. Since Westminster, England is the seat of government in the UK, we adopted the name "House of Lords" for our student government. How cool is that? My senior year, I served as Minister of Exchequer (Treasurer).

those that may have strayed. Student leaders also get an opportunity to represent their groups, meeting with other student leaders prior to competition to review the rules and commit to an honest and fair contest.

I live in a community where agriculture is the prime economic driver, so it makes sense that groups like FFA (Future Farmers of America) and 4-H are popular student groups. The students in FFA undertake impressive yearlong projects, procuring and caring for an animal, training to show it at the fair, and then taking that animal to auction. No matter the weather or their schedule, they need to figure out a way to make sure their animal is cared for and ready to be shown. They are responsible for the development of a living thing, and their financial future depends on how well they do. Talk about responsibility!

Spirit Weeks

Many high school campuses also have spirit weeks, where activities are planned, lunchtime competitions take place, dress up days are coordinated, and a rally and/or dance caps the week off. Sometimes the participants in the activities and competitions are members of a court, like Homecoming or Prom, where candidates for queen and/or king compete for points and student votes. Other times, students are encouraged to develop teams to participate, gathering groups of friends to coordinate outfits, work as a team to overcome lunchtime challenges, and maybe put together some kind of performance at a capstone event at the end of the week. The team that earns the most points at the end of the week is crowned the winner.

The high school where I work has two such weeks, a week in the fall that culminates with Homecoming, and a week in the spring. The Homecoming Week participants are seniors, couples of girls and boys that are candidates for Queen and King of Homecoming. They participate in lunchtime competitions, dress up in the daily theme, perform a dance at the week's end rally, and with the help of their sponsoring club, decorate a float for the parade that precedes the

Homecoming football game. At halftime of the football game we find out who the winners are, and the week culminates with a Homecoming Dance.

No offense to our Homecoming Week participants, but it is our spring spirit week where the real magic happens. During this week, groups of eight to ten students come together to create teams, completing a simple application to participate that includes their individual names, their team's name (which aligns with the week's theme), and a counselor's signature verifying they all have at least a 2.0 GPA. The teams then begin preparing coordinated outfits for the week based on each day's dress up theme, and they begin the process of crafting and rehearsing a routine for the week's culminating event, a lip sync competition. This is my favorite event of the year, one where I get to wow the students with my extraordinary dance skills as a member of the teacher team's exhibition entry into the lip sync. At least I think the students' loud reactions are to my extraordinary dancing.

This week is frenzied, as upwards of fifteen groups of students are coming to school in wildly creative costumes (non-participants dress up too), competing in lunchtime activities, and rehearsing a three to five minute routine to perform at the lip sync. In order to do all of this, students must resourcefully gather a week's worth of outfits that meet specific needs, spend each lunch period competing against other teams in front of the assembled onlookers, spend their evenings crafting and rehearsing an entertaining lip sync routine[5], and then performing that lip sync on a Friday night in front of hundreds of their peers and family members. They do all of this voluntarily, and they do all of it knowing that only one group is going to be crowned the winner, and all they'll get is a medal to hang around their neck and eventually stuff in a box under their bed.

---

[5] A routine which is most often to music snippets that have been spliced together from different songs that represented each day's theme. The creation of this cobbled together song requires the sampling, curation, and then editing of multiple songs into a single file, and most importantly, a group of teenagers coming to a consensus.

And they do all of it by themselves.

Admittedly, there is probably some parent involvement in the outfit part, at minimum by shelling out a few bucks for the students to scour the local thrift stores, but this is almost entirely a student effort, much like my Showcase experience. When I witnessed it for the first time, I instantly made the connection, and have done everything in my power to encourage students to participate. Participation in this one week involves some aspect of all ten challenges, and it requires the development of a huge dose of responsibility. Pulling this whole week off, win or lose, is something any student participant can be proud of, and one that will give them confidence going forward.

Each year, the number of teams that begin the week do not equal the number of teams that end it. While fifteen or sixteen may start, by the time the lip sync rolls around, we may be down to eleven or twelve. The week is demanding, and classes and spring sports do not take a break for this week, so participants are forced to manage the responsibilities of this week on top of all their other responsibilities of homework and practice. The teams fall out at different times and for different reasons, some early in the week due to infighting over costumes or who's going to choreograph the lip sync, some later in the week as the grind just becomes too much and the group disintegrates like an oversaturated paper towel, and some just prior to show time when their lip sync routine just doesn't come together and the thought of public humiliation becomes too much to consider.

These groups, as you can probably imagine, are largely made up of juniors and seniors. They have the confidence to participate because they are aware of what it entails. They have watched it as a freshman and sophomore, they know the work involved, and nothing is a surprise. Often the best team leaders as juniors and seniors got involved when they were a freshman or sophomore, joining a team of upperclassmen, maybe because they had an older sibling on a team. These students that can apprentice when they are young usually evolve into strong leaders later in high school, their teams often in contention for the top overall spot because of their guidance. Upperclassmen are also more independent transportation-wise and having one or more members that can drive makes all the difference when it comes to running around to get outfits and meet for rehearsal. While it has been attempted over the years, we have never had an all-freshman team make it to the end. Valiant groups have tried, but the reliance on parents to drive them around, and the intimidation of performing in an event you have never seen before and have no idea what the norms are, eventually wears them down.

While it appears from the outside, casual observer, to just be an exercise in frivolity, these weeks are magnificent training opportunities for adulthood. Giving students the independence to coordinate, craft, communicate, and compete within the context of a fun activity builds skills and confidence to help them in their transition into adulthood. They generated an interest, they committed the time and effort, they made the sacrifices, they managed their time, they followed through, and they reaped the rewards.

When it all comes together on that glorious Friday evening once a year in the spring, and the gym is packed with students and family members, and electricity is coursing through everyone, likely generated by the teams of students anticipating their performance, I can't help but grin from ear to ear. I am always so excited to watch their performances, and as the lights go down over the crowd and they go up on center court, and the first team launches into their performance, it is always an incredible experience. Their performances are wildly creative, often funny, and always entertaining.

The best moments for me, though, are not the performances themselves, and it is not when the winners are announced. It is the moments just after each performance, when a team is finished with their routine and the crowd reacts with cheers and applause. They hold their final pose, and then break it to look at each other, and that feeling of accomplishment washes over their faces. That is the moment I love. They did it! They did what most others did not or could not. They were on the stage, not in the audience, and adult life just became a little more possible.

Drive, Work, Date, and Save

Face it, your kid's growing up.

During the high school years, many students will experience some of life's important coming of age moments: learning to drive and earning their driver's license, applying for and obtaining their first job, going on a date with someone they have feelings for, and opening a bank account. All these events, when they happen during high school with support from parents and while their peers are also experiencing them, begin to develop a sense that adulthood is possible. They experience being responsible for executing tasks reserved for the more mature among us and, in doing so, become comfortable with moving forward. This is like entering the ocean from the beach, gradually, safely. Students that put these moments off set themselves up for a cliff dive. Or better yet, parents that do not allow these things to happen are chaperones for the journey to the cliff and are likely to be dragged off it by their frightened children.

I am amazed at how many young people today do not obtain a driver's license. I understand there are financial considerations, like the cost of a driver's training program your state may require. I also understand that once they obtain the license, the expenses continue to pile up in the form of increased insurance, gas, and vehicle maintenance. And in some areas, like in large metropolitan cities like New York, it might not make sense. But even in all those situations, if it is at all possible, I would encourage every high school teenager to pursue their license.

The days of high schools offering the classroom and driving portions of the driver training program are disappearing (if not entirely gone) where you live. But, to fill the void, young people can now do the classroom portion of driver training on their phone through an app, and it's usually pretty cheap (I think my son's was less than $50, maybe less than $30). They still must get behind the wheel for a minimum number of hours with a licensed trainer, and they most likely also need to practice with a family member for a suggested number of hours. But what great training to be an adult! Getting behind the wheel of a large machine and navigating the streets, adjusting for other drivers and traffic lights, all the while obeying the rules is a massive undertaking. It is a moment I am sure all of us remember vividly, the first time we pulled a car into traffic and were fully responsible for its movements. But look where we all are now, safely wading in the ocean, comfortable and confident. Putting it off only makes the cliff steeper and higher.

Driver's licenses come in handy for that first job. The act of applying for, interviewing, obtaining, and then working at an establishment that will compensate them for their efforts, is a rite of passage. Is there anything more adult than working? It is the defining characteristic of about a forty-year chunk of our life and learning how to do it before the pressure to use the money to pay bills kicks in is important. It also exposes students to different types of jobs, like retail sales, manual labor, working with kids, or maybe even working with animals. They will need to manage their time and deal with customers. They will have a boss they may or may not care for. Dealing with co-workers will be a positive or negative experience, or maybe both. Going out and being a contributing member of the workforce is a great experience for a young person, and it feels especially good when they get that first paycheck.

Something they might want to do with that money is ask someone out on a date. Equipped with a driver's license and money, a teenager is primed to experience the iconic life moment of going out with someone they are interested in or maybe already have a relationship with. On a typical date, a teenager is likely to experience making plans for what to do, communicating those plans, driving and meeting other parents, making reservations at a restaurant, ordering food from a waiter, eating and making conversation, paying the bill and (hopefully) calculating an appropriate tip, and navigating any of the awkward and intense emotions associated with a date. As they sit there at dinner, just the two of them (or maybe it is a group date), and they look around the restaurant they are likely to see adults doing the same thing. In that moment they feel another wave of "I can do this," a belief that the transition to adulthood is possible.

In order to pay for this date with money from their job, a bank account is probably needed. Opening a bank account for your teenager while they are in high school is a great idea. The account might need to be linked to yours depending on their age, but that is good because it allows for easy transfer of funds. Along with the bank account, obtaining a debit card that allows them to access those funds is good training (dangerous, but necessary). The act of depositing a paycheck, withdrawing cash, and using a debit card to make a purchase are all very adult actions. This will also force budgeting, and the more guidance they can receive on this the better. Learning how to save and allocate discretionary money to make sure money is available for things like gas or a burger out with friends is great practice. Also, not being able to join their friends for a burger because they bought new shoes is a great way to learn about making choices with money.

The more these very important adult activities are delayed, the more likely they become bigger and scarier than they need to be. This is true of most things we avoid for various reasons, becoming more difficult to accomplish the longer we wait. Becoming a responsible adult requires teenagers to accept that becoming an adult is something they can handle, look forward to even. By dipping their toes in the water with entry-level adult activities like driving, working, dating, and banking, young people can start to envision a world where they are a thriving adult. Delaying these activities can delay their transition to adulthood.

Just being "academically" ready for life is not enough.

Wrapping It Up

When Michael Phelps speaks about being a hyperactive, novice child swimmer in Baltimore, one of the details he shares is that some of the older swimmers in the club he swam for qualified for the Olympics. To the young Michael Phelps, qualifying for the Olympics was not unrealistic. Swimmers in his club did it, and so could he. The rest is history.

Making the future real is a big part of making the future happen. There is always going to be a part of us that is unsure, nervous, or even afraid. It is unknown, and it is something we want. The more we can help our teenagers see adult life as tangible, as something they can slide into and be welcomed, the better. One of the greatest fears young people experience as they approach adulthood is that they will be seen as a fraud, an imposter. It is a terrible feeling to think everyone is staring at you because you do not know the rules, and your movements and your words are those of a child, not an adult. It is enough to keep many from trying to join the party in the first place.

By helping our teenagers accept more and more responsibility for their own lives, the more we ensure a gentle descent into the deep waters of adulthood. By getting involved in activities that require them to lead, like yearbook, student government, or service clubs, students can start to become comfortable with responsibility. By stepping into leadership positions in their organizations, like sports or music, young people become apprentice adults, their coaches and supervisors deputizing them to handle organization business. By accepting the challenge of earning a driver's license and driving on city streets, getting a job and earning money, going on a date and calculating a tip, and depositing a paycheck and allocating a portion to savings, teenagers start to feel like an adult. With help at first, and then independently, they start to move about in society of their own free will and volition. The more they do it, the more comfortable they become, the more responsibility they are ready to take on.

Like the quote that leads off this chapter insinuates, liberty demands the free to be responsible. If we do not want our teenagers to dread it, and we do not want them to stand on the cliff's edge and walk backwards, then we need to help them find the beach and enjoy a safe entry.

The Tenth Challenge: HANDLE RESPONSIBILITY

The Challenge's Impact on Trajectories

Ready for Take Off!

They are ready! The best that we can hope for is this, that our child is ready and willing to accept the responsibilities of life, and they have the confidence and skills to back it up. They confidently interact with other adults, feeling like a true member of the club. Confidence in their membership also allows them to seek help when they need it, knowing that this does not betray their status, something that is not in question, but instead is itself an adult quality. Their increasing comfort with responsibility allows them to grow their capacity and handle more of it, which leads to advances in the workplace and beyond. Their responsible money management allows them to grow their wealth and accept larger responsibilities, like home ownership, well before their less responsible peers. Their responsible life management also makes them a more attractive life partner, attracting higher quality suitors. Stability, the outcome of responsible life management, allows them to experience greater growth in all areas because their focus can be on growing and building, and not constantly fixing and replacing. A happy life begins with taking responsibility, and that is exactly what these students have accomplished.

Still Boarding

Our late bloomers need a little more time before they are ready for full submersion into adulthood. They may be caught in a hybrid situation, with a good job that is paying them well, but they're still living at home because they sunk all of their money into a ridiculously large truck and are having trouble gathering a deposit for their own place. In some ways, they may be very much an adult, like utilizing their great communication skills to be the top salesman on the floor, but their video game addiction is keeping them locked in a dark room with a headset on, instead of attending actual social settings and developing relationships with other adults instead of avatars. They are up to their waist in water, and they have taken a long pause knowing that the next move, submerging the torso, will be the most shocking. They will get there, eventually, hopefully. It might take meeting the right person, or maybe the right job. It might take an event that forces them to step up and be a leader, and in doing so instills a confidence that will dislodge them and get them moving forward again. There is a danger that the big truck and high end video game system hold them back, and while we want our children to know that they are always welcome home, we want to make sure we're not holding them back by making it too easy for them to stay.

Flight Delayed

Our poor students that failed to develop their capacity for handling responsibility by avoiding it at all costs, by always choosing to sit in the audience instead of getting involved, find themselves on the cliff's edge. The jump into adulthood is too frightening, the fall too far, the contact with the surface too bracing to imagine. So instead they stand, frozen, staring off at the adults in the distance, frolicking and thriving in their new environment. They will retreat from the cliff's edge and find a safe space where the only responsibilities that exist, like "pull on sweats" and "power up game system," are about all that they can handle. Work is going to be hard to come by, or at least hard to hold onto if their ability to handle a range of responsibilities— proper grooming standards for work, proper attire, show up on time, do designated task for hours, follow interaction protocols with guests and co-workers, take breaks at set times and for set lengths—isn't something they're capable of. If they do find work and hold onto it, it may sap all their energy for responsible behavior, leading to a life of irresponsible behavior beyond the workday.

PD for Parents & Teachers

For Parents

- Systematically increasing the amount of responsibilities your teenager has around the house as they progress through high school will build their capacity for handling all that life demands. Realistic expectations for their academic performance remain, but household chore responsibilities can increase as their skills increase. It takes training, and a lot of patience, but they're only going to be a responsible adult that can buy groceries and cook, clean the bathroom, do laundry, and take care of the yard if they learn how to do them and that they can do them.

- Support money management by establishing a monthly allowance and helping your teen create a budget to meet their monthly needs. If you are constantly reaching into your wallet and handing over cash, they will have difficulty understanding how planning and their choices are important aspects of managing money in life. Take the time to think off all of the items your child needs money for in a month for regular expenses—gas in the car, lunch money, going to the movies with friends—and come up with an amount that you give them at the start of the month. Help them make a budget, allocate the funds (maybe using the envelope method, by putting some in an envelope labeled "gas," some more in one labeled "lunch," and the rest in the "fun" envelope), and then allow them to experience the pains of mis-management. This means you have to be willing to drive them to school, or maybe have them walk or beg their friends for a ride, when they spend their "gas" money on new speakers for their car (which can lead to a lesson on saving for large purchases).

- Support them and encourage them in doing adult activities like driving, getting a job, and opening a bank account. Holding them back because you are afraid, or because you want them to intensely focus on their studies is doing them a disservice. Being academically ready for life is not being ready for life. Life is so much more than being smart and having a college degree. This planet is littered with smart people that fail miserably at life because they cannot handle the simplest of responsibilities, like paying bills on time or checking for expiration dates on food. We want to develop young people that can imagine themselves as adults in all facets of life, and that takes getting their nose out of their books and getting them into the world.

For Teachers

- Get to know your campus and all its events and organizations. Be a fountain of knowledge and information for your students, making regular announcements, daily even, of opportunities for students to get involved in activities and groups that will help them build responsibility. Dedicate a bulletin board to posters and announcements that students can look at on their way in or out of their classroom. Utilize electronic communications tools, like Remind or Google Classroom to communicate stuff like application deadlines or club meeting dates and locations. Once you know your students, make targeted suggestions to students when opportunities to get involved in something that matches their interest comes up.
- Model responsible behavior by being prepared for class each day, by staying on top of your grading, and by maintaining an orderly classroom. Teacher credibility is a high impact facet of what we do, and if we're going to demand that our students be responsible for maintaining an orderly binder, for meeting deadlines, and for showing up prepared for class each day, we need to do the same. There is nothing that sours credibility more, and with it our ability to connect with and inspire young

211

people to improve, than the hypocritical teacher (hypocritical *anything*, really) that demands behavior that they themselves do not exhibit.

- Teach responsibility, do not just expect it. Set up responsible systems and expectations, make it clear how to meet the expectations, model it, practice it, and then be the warm demander that accepts nothing less. If your expectation is that they always write the question and the answer on their paper, and you've made this clear and modeled it, and a student turns a paper with the answers only, hand it back to them and gently remind them of the expectation. Do not get put off by eye rolls, and do not engage in an argument over why. Just be a broken record, repeat your expectations, and ask them to do it properly. They will come to realize that doing it right the first time is so much easier.

Habits that Work for Teenagers

- **Every day when I get home from school, I will plug my phone into the charger and complete any chores I have.** By developing a habit that promotes doing their household responsibilities over hopping on the game system or plopping on their bed and spiraling into social media land, teenagers develop the ability to prioritize. Eventually they will need to be able to prioritize paying the utilities bill over buying a new purse or cleaning the bathroom over watching the football game.

- **Whenever a friend gets a job, I will ask them how they got it and what their responsibilities are.** Part of becoming an adult is transitioning from parents and other adults as the main source of information and moving to a reliable peer group that can provide support and valuable insight. When friends they know and trust experience something before they do, like getting a job or earning a driver's license, not only is the process demystified, but it makes it seem possible. If they can do it, so can I!

- **Whenever volunteers are asked for, I will offer my services.** People are always asking for help, and individuals generally respond in one of two ways, regardless of the request: with "I can help," or a diversion of the eyes. Helping others is not only the right thing to do, but it's an opportunity in a low stakes way (expectations are always less when you're doing something for free) to learn how to handle responsibility and possibly develop a new skill. Developing this reaction, to offer help when needed instead of avoiding extra work, will pay so many dividends in life.

Conclusion:
A CALL to ACTION

We must all face the choice between what is right and what is easy.

From *Harry Potter and the Goblet of Fire* by J.K. Rowling

The world is counting on us.

When my wife Laurie and I sat down to craft our vision for the entity that eventually became our website, blog, podcast, and this book (find details for everything in the appendix), the truth is we didn't need to. We are both fiftyish year-old veteran teachers that have managed our money well and have been able to carve out a nice little life in California's Central Valley. We have two beautiful and rapidly growing teenagers that are both extremely active, with most of our evenings and weekends composed of travel to practices, parent meetings, high school games, and weekend tournaments, many of which require travel and hotel stays. We have always felt so lucky to be a two-teacher family that enjoys the same schedule as our children, and we have taken advantage of those extended times off together to travel to some of our favorite places. While we live in a fairly sleepy, smallish town, we're just over a two hour drive to Los Angeles, and Laurie and I relish the opportunity to drive down occasionally to catch our favorite bands in concert, U2, Coldplay, and

Paul McCartney[1] among our recent highlights. And, oh yeah, we both work full time, and both take on extra responsibilities at our school. So, we are busy as it is, and our combined income from teaching is sufficient for the life we desire.

The truth is, we began this project because we felt compelled to.

Prior to our relocation to our current town, Laurie and I had lived and worked as teachers in both Southern California and Hawaii. I am a product of Southern California's Orange County, and Laurie grew up on the beautiful island of Oahu, Hawaii's most populous island and home to world famous Honolulu, Waikiki, and Pearl Harbor. Both locations are bustling hubs that enjoy a constant flux of new transplants. People from all over the country and planet relocate to these places for their ideal weather and business opportunities. I cannot tell you how many times we heard the story, "I came here on vacation and never left!" We both enjoyed the energy these places created, and while the traffic can at times be a pain, we saw it as a worthy tradeoff for everything we got in return. When our daughter was born, we decided to move for financial reasons. It was a difficult decision, because we really love Hawaii, and the private school where we taught was a dream place to work, but with now two children to care for, and two measly private school teacher incomes in very expensive-to-live Hawaii (at the time, milk was routinely $7 per gallon), the desire for some of life's simpler desires like a second car and a second bathroom (not to mention a college savings plan), forced our move off of the island. We settled in California's Central Valley because Laurie had some family in the area, it was just a short drive to our old haunts and my family in Southern California, and it was incredibly less expensive to live than anywhere we'd been before.

When we finally settled into the teaching positions at the high school Laurie and I have worked at for over a decade now, a realization washed over us. Our new hometown was largely populated with people that grew up in that town. There were very few transplants. This hit us when we

---

[1] The most recent time we saw Sir Paul was at Dodger Stadium, where Ringo Starr joined him on stage during the encore for Sgt. Pepper's Lonely Hearts Club Band and Helter Skelter!

were at a staff meeting and everyone was sharing where they went to high school. We were the staff of a newly opened high school, the third in our town, and almost everyone had graduated from one of the other two. Those that did not had graduated from one of the high schools in a neighboring town twenty minutes north, and still lived there and commuted in.

Never had we felt like such outsiders. Not in a bad way, like we were not accepted, but in a way that said they all have a shared past that we are not a part of. In our previous locations, we worked with people from all over the country, and in Hawaii, from all over the world. It was odd to be from those areas. In places like that, where there is not a shared history among the assembled, it was easy to believe your ability to make large-scale impact as a teacher was minimal. These are global way stations, with swirling and constantly changing populations. How much of a difference can I really make?

In our new location, we felt the exact opposite; The town's future depended on us.

After the initial shock of feeling like an outsider fell away, it hit us that every future resident of this town, every future adult, home builder, policeman, nurse, gardener, and chef were in our classrooms. If I wanted to make sure that my home was safely constructed, the streets were safe for my children, that I'd receive proper care when I got sick, that the plants in my yard looked beautiful, and that the meals I ate when I enjoyed a dinner out were delicious, then I needed to do a great job. The power of teachers to save the world every day (hence the name for our project) through their efforts hit us like a ton of bricks at that moment, in a way it never had before. All the future adult residents of our town were sitting in our classrooms. Their knowledge and skill development were our responsibility. Their character was being developed on our campus, and as they say, character is destiny.

While I use the word "teacher" here in reference to my job title, I have come to understand it is not an exclusive title. Anyone that teaches is a teacher, and parents are the largest single group of teachers on the planet. Coaches, pastors, instructors, directors, and anyone else involved in the business of helping young people learn how to be decent human beings with some skills to transition to adulthood and become productive, contributing members of society is a teacher. So, regardless of how you make your money, odds are you are a teacher.

And the world depends on you, on us.

"I'm Not Getting Paid for This"

I have always despised the phrase, "I'm not getting paid for this." Whenever it leaves someone's lips, I know what is likely to follow. There is going to be some excuse as to why they are not doing a better job. Somehow the lack of financial compensation not only means that their best effort should not be expected, but that whatever pitiful effort is being given, we should be profusely thankful for it. If I have any influence on the staffing decisions, that phrase is an instant signal that it is time to part ways.

I remember early in my teaching life I was reading an article that outlined the twelve characteristics of the best and most effective teachers. One of the characteristics has always stuck in my head: the best teachers saw teaching as a "calling," rather than a "career," and not as a "job." In my experience, most of the teachers I have worked with check this box. It is common wisdom that nobody goes into teaching for the money, especially if you live in a particularly expensive area. When Laurie and I got our first teaching jobs, we were in Southern California, one of our country's more expensive places to live. While friends of ours were pursuing more lucrative careers, we felt compelled to work with young people knowing that our compensation would mean we would probably never live in the nicest neighborhoods or drive the nicest cars. We taught because we felt we had to, and anything else at that time just did not seem sufficient. We both felt so alive when we made the decision! It has been at the center of our life for the last couple decades, and we could not imagine having done anything else.

I know now that the idea of seeing what you do as a calling, as something much greater than just a paycheck, makes you the best and most efficient *anything*. It does not just apply to teaching. The feeling that you were put on this earth to do what you get paid to do is something we all aspire to. I do not have such a Pollyanna view of life as to suggest you should quit your job if it is just a paycheck and go find something that lights your fire every day, because life's too short! I am more of a pragmatist than an idealist, and I understand life requires us to make certain sacrifices to make ends meet.

But I do adhere to the belief that no matter what we choose to do in life, especially when that choice involves another person's development, giving anything less than our best effort is a crime. This is why teachers that perceive their job to be a calling, similar to how a priest may express his desire to enter the clergy as responding to a direct request, a call, from the heavens, are considered among the most effective in their field. Someone that believes that deeply about their profession is always going to give it their all. Likewise, if we make a choice, even if that choice is as a volunteer knowing that there will not be a paycheck as compensation for your efforts, giving anything less than your best hurts us all. It really hurts when it involves young people.

Early in the book I shared with you how I felt almost ashamed by how much I was exposed to and learned about families through the students I taught. Metaphorically getting to peer through windows into the living rooms of so many households, you start to understand the raw power of adults' influence over young people and their development. Not that this was a revelation, but maybe a reshaping of an earlier belief that despite the circumstances of life, a person can become what they dream. I still believe this in theory, but I also know that the adults that surround that person, and the effort they give or don't give to their development, play a huge role in just how challenging the realization of that dream is going to be.

I know this may sound like I am stating the obvious, but sometimes we need to be reminded of our awesome power and responsibility to shape the future through our work with young people. Our children, students, players, cast members, and neighbors are counting on us to give our best effort, regardless of our compensation. If you do not already have the mindset, effort must be given to shifting how you see your work with young people as a calling, as a planet saving mission. They, the young people we work with, will ultimately need to be the ones to conquer the challenges. We cannot and should not overplay our hand when they begin their journey, their hero's journey, through high school. It is their quest, not ours, but like Gandolf to Frodo, we play an important role.

A cobbled-together directive from *The Teenage Brain* by Frances E. Jensen, MD with Amy Ellis Nutt:

The teen years are a great time to test where a kid's strengths are, and to even out weaknesses that need attention...Your teenagers won't always accept your advice, but you can't give it unless you're trying to understand how they're learning...At the end of the day, your kids still have to grow up and develop and learn and mature on their own. You can't do it for them...You will have to invest more time and effort in your teen than you probably ever anticipated. You are the parent...You want to always remain as positive as you can because you want to empower your teenagers and help them understand what an amazing time of their lives this is, a time of opportunity. Your job isn't to stifle them but rather to help them channel their energies in positive directions.

Peace of Mind

I still, after all these years, have a part of me that is downright delusional. This insane part of me believes that at some point down the road, usually just around the corner and out of sight, life is going to get easier. Once I round the bend, there is an area where I finally get to pull off the road and take a break. The traffic disappears, the scenery is beautiful and serene, the weather perfect, and I am surrounded by all my favorite people and things. For me, this area is coastal, where the salty smell of the ocean is always there in trace amounts, becoming thicker the closer you draw near the shore. This place has a great movie house that's always showing something Laurie and I want to go see, and a funky little live music venue that always seems to have bands playing that are on the verge of making it big. Even after they make it big, they like to come back and play for the locals on the small stage, seeking to recapture some of that energy they had when they were fighting to get bigger. There is a casual spot that serves great craft beer and burgers that is always busy, but the wait is never long. The servers all wear colorful aloha shirts and shorts, and the setting sun can be seen slipping into the ocean from the patio where we always eat. My wife and kids are with me on the patio, and there is no bickering, just deep, thought provoking conversation interrupted with bouts of genuine, gut busting laughter. After dinner we usually walk over to the bookstore nearby that also has a great selection of vinyl records and magazines. We all split off and go to our favorite areas, browsing the shelves, checking out the staff recommendations, perusing the sale table, and flipping through the magazines. We never make a plan, but somehow we always finish our journey through the store at the same time, meeting up at the checkout counter with our various items, those books and records and magazines that piqued our interest and will shape our thinking over the next few weeks while we digest them, until the next time we can repeat this process. With our heavy bags in tow, we walk to our final destination through the balmy, dark, and moonlit air, laughter and music spilling out from the venues nearby. We enter the brightly lit, white tiled ice cream shop and order our favorite concoctions, the girls and I getting something chocolatey and blended, our favorite chunks of baked sweets like treasure to be discovered with our long spoons. My son will get a shake, preferring to suck down his treat, the straw entering his mouth from the side, at an angle. Once done, we pile in the car for the short drive home, excitedly placing our new purchases where they belong: the books on our nightstands, the records piled next to the record player (they'll be filed away with the other records *after* they get played), and the magazines on various side tables in the living room.

What makes this moment "easier" is not that it is casual, or fun, or free of work. It's not even that it seems to be free of impending work, like a Friday or Saturday night when you know you have nothing pressing to get up for the next morning and the alarm can be turned off. It is not even that there might never be work in the morning ever again, like in retirement, where each day is a creation of your own making and not at least partially dictated by someone else's needs[2]. No, it is something more than that. Having a great burger, finding a great book, engaging in great conversation with loved ones, and ending the night with a great sweet treat and going to bed knowing you get to wake up when you're ready to are all things that make us feel good, but they're momentary. The memories stay with us, sure, and the ideas and information we may have gleaned from the books or records may become new and permanent residents of our brain, but again they just made life better and not necessarily easier.

The truth is, life does not get easier, especially if you have and or work with children, no matter their age. But everything I just described[3], is just a really nice day. I always get deepest in my delusions when life seems particularly difficult, that kind of grind that seems to sap every last bit of your capacity to handle everything you're being asked to juggle, leaving only time for sleep before it's repeated. But as soon as the challenges lighten, and there is more and more room for gardening and reading, I get wistful for the grind. The journey is challenging, but it is also energizing and life affirming. There is a reason it is not referred to as a Hero's *Destination*; life is all about the journey.

What makes all of this, this ideal life "easier," is not that somehow the work ends and we get to take a break (because as parents and teachers it never will), it's that we know we did our best to become the best we

---

[2] Note: this description of retirement was penned by someone not in retirement and represents the idea of retirement from someone who knows nothing about it. If you are retired, forgive this fool for he knows not what he says.

[3] Which I realized as I was writing was my description of heaven, just as my dad had described his to me, causing the floodgates to open, which is overwhelming for us men that are less skilled emotionally.

are capable of becoming. If I can someday eat and drink with my family as I watch the sun go down, shop for some great books and records, enjoy just a tad too much ice cream, and then head home knowing I did my best to be the best father, teacher, and husband I was capable of becoming, then that might be when my delusions go away. Until then, I will keep working, learning, growing, struggling, and adjusting.

I challenge you to join me. Our teenagers need us.

The world is counting on us.

Acknowledgments

In his lovely book *Steal Like an Artist*, Austin Kleon notes, "You are, in fact, a mashup of what you choose to let into your life. You are the sum of your influences." I could not agree more.

This book represents over two decades of my influences, from the people I have known to the publications I have read. They've all, in some way, shaped my thoughts and understandings of education, high school, teaching, parenting, learning, maturing, and what it means to be a teenager. It is a process that thankfully never ends. It is my continual Hero's Journey.

While it is impossible for me to acknowledge every voice or idea that trickled through my granite skull and contributed to the well I drew from to write this book, it would be criminal for me not to try. Here goes.

Without my wife, Laurie Jones, I am not an author. I am probably not a lot of things, chief among them married, a father, happy, and relatively healthy, body, mind, and soul. If we are twin reservoirs set side by side, mine sits a few inches beneath yours, gravity continually sending your overflow of grace, love, wisdom, and joy spilling into my damaged and leaking pool. You have been my inspiration and best friend for almost half of my life, tirelessly and without pause reading and editing every single line of text I have composed for *anything* for over twenty years. 100% of the proceeds of this and any other book I am lucky enough to publish in my lifetime will not come close to repaying you for your bottomless time and patience. "I love you, forever," and the occasional dinner at Dukes will hopefully suffice.

For the last decade and a half, I have also had the humbling joy of being a father to my son, October, and my daughter, London[1]. You are

---

[1] Give us a break, our last name is Jones. Odds are, you know a "Matt Jones," and it is not me. But do you know an October or London Jones?

Acknowledgments

entering your senior and freshman year of high school as I type this, and I hope that I have been half the mentor I try to inspire others to be. I have learned so much from both of you, even though I am not the best at letting you know that. You both give purpose to every early morning writing session, every heart-pounding rowing machine rep, and every weekend spent pool or courtside at some high school four hours away. You make all the effort worth it. I love you.

To my mother, Peggy "Nanna" Jones, and mother-in-law, Mae "Vava" Bush, for your many hours around the dinner table listening to me blather on about this idea or that, and then having the patience to read my manuscript and offer feedback...thank you.

To my late father, Curt Jones, who taught me the value of continued growth, and that it is never too late to write your book...thank you.

To my brother, Lucas Jones, for joining me on stage and in the classroom, and for always supplying a steady and energetic beat...thank you.

To two friends and colleagues, Doug Jones and Diane Reis, that gave me so much more valuable insight and feedback than I could have ever asked for...thank you.

To friend and colleague "J Yav" for the huge assist with the cover art...thank you.

To the other friends, Michaelpaul Mendoza, Lynn Roberts, and Alycia King, who read an early draft and supplied me with important edits and revisions...thank you.

To my professors and classmates in both the CSU Long Beach Multiple Subject Credential program (2002) and the CSU Fresno MAT, Multicultural and Social Justice program (2015)...thank you.

To the teachers and administrators I've learned from at Warner Middle School (Westminster, CA), Le Jardin Academy (Kailua, HI), Lee Richmond Elementary (Hanford, CA), Sunnyside Union (Strathmore, CA), and Mission Oak High School (Tulare, CA)...thank you.

And finally, to every student I have ever had at any of those fine institutions. You have all been influences on my life, and you have all contributed to the lessons received by those that came after you. My life has been a worthwhile journey because of the time I've been able to spend with you, hearing your stories, watching you grow, being frustrated by the unnecessary barriers you've had put in your way, and by watching you crash through them every time. I am very lucky to have been allowed to be your teacher for one year of your life...thank you.

Bibliography

Allen, D. (2001). *Getting Things Done: The Art of Stress-Free Productivity*. New York. Penguin Books.

Brown, P. C., Roediger III, H. L., McDaniel, M. A., (2014) *Make it Stick: The Science of Successful Learning*. Cambridge, MA. Harvard University Press

Carey, B. (2014) *How We Learn: The Surprising Truth About When, Where, and Why It Happens*. New York. Random House.

Carr, N. (2011). *The Shallows: What The Internet is Doing to Our Brains*. New York. Norton.

Duckworth, A. (2016). *Grit: The Power and Passion of Perseverance*. New York. Scribner.

Duhigg, C. (2012). *The Power of Habit: Why We Do What We Do in Life and Work*. New York. Random House.

Dweck, C. S., (2006). *Mindset: The New Psychology of Success*. New York. Ballantine.

Epstein, D. (2019). *Range: Why Generalists Triumph in a Specialized World*. New York. Riverhead Books.

Foer, J. (2012). *Moonwalking With Einstein: The Art and Science of Remembering Everything*. New York. Penguin Books.

Heath, D. (2020). *Upstream: The Quest to Solve Problems Before They Happen*. New York. Avid Reader Press.

Jensen, F. E., and Nutt, A. E. (2015). *The Teenage Brain: A Neuroscientist's Survival Guide to Raising Adolescents and Young Adults*. New York. Harper.

Kleon, A. (2012). *Steal Like an Artist: 10 Things Nobody Told You About Being Creative*. New York. Workman.

McConville, M. (2020). *Failure to Launch: Why Your Twentysomething Hasn't Grown Up...and What to Do About It*. New York. Putnam.

Medina, J. (2014) *Brain Rules: 12 Principles for Surviving and Thriving at Work, Home, and School*. Seattle, WA. Pear Press.

Oakley, B. (2014) *A Mind for Numbers: How to Excel at Math and Science Even if You Flunked Algebra*. New York. Tarcher/Penguin.

Willingham, D. T., (2009) *Why Don't Students Like School: A Cognitive Scientist Answers Questions About How The Mind Works and What It Means for the Classroom*. San Francisco. Jossey Bass.